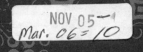
NOV 05—1
Mar. 06=10

GLEN ELLYN PUBLIC LIBRARY

3 1322 00447 4863

W9-CCL-402

handknit HOLIDAYS

handknit

KNITTING YEAR-ROUND FOR CHRISTMAS, HANUKKAH, AND WINTER SOLSTICE

HOLIDAYS

Melanie Falick *with* Betty Christiansen

photographs by Susan Pittard

GLEN ELLYN PUBLIC LIBRARY
400 DUANE STREET
GLEN ELLYN, ILLINOIS 60137

STC CRAFT | A MELANIE FALICK BOOK   NEW YORK

For Ben, who brings so much light—and sparkle—into my life.

Text copyright © 2005 Melanie Falick

Photographs copyright © 2005 Susan Pittard

All rights reserved. No portion of this book may be reproduced, stored in a retrieval system, or transmitted in any form or by any means, mechanical, electronic, photocopying, recording, or otherwise, without written permission from the publisher.

Published in 2005 by
STC Craft | A Melanie Falick Book
115 West 18th Street
New York, NY 10011
www.abramsbooks.com

Canadian Distribution:
Canadian Manda Group
165 Dufferin Street
Toronto, Ontario M6K 3HG
Canada

Library of Congress Cataloging-in-Publication Data
Falick, Melanie.
Handknit holidays : knitting year-round for Christmas, Hanukkah, and winter solstice /
Melanie Falick with Betty Christiansen ; photographs by Susan Pittard.
p. cm.
Includes index.
ISBN 1-58479-454-2
1. Knitting--Patterns. 2. Christmas decorations. 3. Hanukkah decorations.
I. Christiansen, Betty. II. Title.
TT825.F3497 2005
746.43'2041—dc22
2004026283

Design: woolypear
Production: Jane Searle
The text of this book was composed in Mrs Eaves and Helvetica Neue.

Printed in China

10 9 8 7 6 5 4 3 2 1

First Printing

Stewart, Tabori & Chang is a subsidiary of
LA MARTINIÈRE GROUPE

CONTENTS

Christmas, Hanukkah, Kwanzaa, Winter Solstice—just about everyone has something to celebrate in December. *Handknit Holidays* was created with these occasions in mind. An eclectic collection of more than fifty gifts, decorations, and clothing pieces, it is meant to bring fresh ideas and new traditions to these special days.

The projects in *Handknit Holidays* were designed by thirty different people, each of whom puts her unique stamp on the holiday season. Some of the projects reflect particular family or cultural traditions; others are brand-new ideas based upon other influences. When I originally presented this book's concept to the designers, many responded enthusiastically to the possibility of celebrating the winter solstice, feeling it was a refreshing way to escape some of the commercial trappings of the season while still embracing the holiday spirit. As I gathered their finished pieces and pondered how we would present them, I kept thinking about "taking back" these holidays, reclaiming them from the marketers who try to lure us into a commercial whirl every year. I fantasized instead about a holiday season full of unique handcrafts, especially handknits, ranging from classic to trendy, old-fashioned to modern, conservative to quirky—anything our imaginations could dream up—and, of course, plenty of time for the making. For me, this would be joyful!

I hope the projects in this book, as well as the way they are presented, bring that sense of joy to you, inspiring you to pick up your needles year-round, create wonderful things, and, in the process, conjure up some fresh holiday spirit. For, while giving a handknit is an act of kindness toward someone else, isn't making a handknit a gift to ourselves? Especially during the holiday season, I treasure any time I can spend creating something with my hands, sometimes quietly on my own and other times while socializing with family and friends. Like pausing on the winter solstice to appreciate the beauty of the changing seasons—and to feel some relief knowing that from this point on the days will lengthen—when I stop to knit, I feel a sense of peace often missing when I'm charging around the mall or winding my way through holiday traffic. I also begin to feel revitalized when I'm knitting, ready to bake more cookies, sign more cards, even put on a party dress.

When it comes down to it, knitting for these year-end occasions gives me a chance to recapture the essence of the holidays: peace, joy, and rejuvenation. I hope it does for you as well. And I hope this book helps you to remember—

'Tis the season to be . . . knitting!

Melanie

DECK THE HALLS

Designs for the Home

LEIGH RADFORD *Knitted and Felted Ornaments and Garland*

The tradition of decorating a tree for Christmas is universal, though every culture has its own twist. In Scandinavia, ornaments may be woven from straw; Eastern Europe is famous for handpainted eggs; and those in Japan who decorate Christmas trees do so with tiny fans, paper lanterns, and origami swans. Here, Leigh Radford uses wool. In one version, her ornaments are simple balls knit in solid colors or stripes (see left). In the other, colored fleece is felted into small balls that are joined and embellished in myriad ways—even strung together into a garland (see pages 12 and 13).

Knitted Ornaments

FINISHED MEASUREMENTS
Small (Large): Approximately 3 (4 ¼)" diameter

YARN
Harrisville Highland Style (100% wool; 200 yards / 100 grams): 1 skein each #4 gold, #17 Bermuda blue, #16 teal blue, #22 plum, #7 tundra (gold/green), #48 dove gray, #38 teak (brown)

NEEDLES
One set of five double-pointed needles (dpn) size US 7 (4.5 mm)
Change needle size if necessary to obtain correct gauge.

NOTIONS
Crochet hook size F/5 (3.75 mm)
Polyester batting, yarn needle

GAUGE
24 sts and 28 rows = 4" (10 cm) in Stockinette stitch (St st)

Note: Work ornaments in solid colors or in stripes, as desired.

CO 12 (20) sts; distribute sts evenly over 4 needles—3 (5) sts each needle.
Join for working in the rnd, being careful not to twist sts; place marker (pm) for beginning of rnd.

Bottom
Rnd 1: Knit.
Rnd 2: [K1-f/b, knit across to last st on needle, k1-f/b] 4 times—20 (28) sts.
Repeat Rnds 1 and 2 until there are 11 (15) sts on each needle—44 (60) sts.
Work even for 5 (9) rnds.

Top
Rnd 1: [Skp, knit across to last 2 sts on needle, k2tog] 4 times—36 (52) sts remain.
Rnd 2: Knit.
Repeat Rnds 1 and 2 until 3 (5) sts remain on each needle, end after completing Rnd 2—12 (20) sts remain.
Break yarn, leaving an 18" tail. With tail threaded onto yarn needle, slip sts onto tail—DO NOT gather at this point.

Finishing
Using CO tail threaded on yarn needle, weave yarn through CO edge; gently pull to gather closed. Weave in end securely on WS. Stuff ornament with batting. Gather live sts at BO edge and gently pull to close opening. Using BO tail and crochet hook, work a 4½" chain; fasten off, leaving a tail for attaching chain to ball. Secure end of chain to top of ornament to form a loop. Embellish ornaments with embroidery if desired.

Felted Ornaments and Garland

FINISHED MEASUREMENTS
Small (Large): approximately $\frac{1}{2}$ (1)" diameter

FLEECE
Harrisville Fleece (100% wool): 1 ounce each
#4 gold, #17 Bermuda blue, #16 teal blue,
#22 plum, #7 tundra, #45 dove gray, #38 teak,
#8 hemlock

MATERIALS
Felting needle (available at yarn stores
and from Harrisville Design; see Sources
for Supplies, page 182)
Pan or tub for water, dishwashing soap,
rubber gloves with textured palms (for friction
and faster felting)
Leather lacing—18 feet or desired length
for garland; 8–10" for each ornament
Yarn needle, sequin pins, seed beads—size 11
or smaller works best (bead must be small
enough not to slip off the head of the pin),
craft glue

Solid-Color Felt Balls
Working close to a sink, fill pan or tub with a
couple inches of very hot, soapy water.
Select a small section of fleece in desired
color—filling the palm of your hand. Put on rubber gloves, tear fleece into small sections,
and begin to roll the pieces together in a circular
fashion between your palms. Dip the fleece into
the hot, soapy water and continue to roll the
now wet fleece in your hands, adding additional
pieces of torn fleece if you would like to increase
the size of the ball. Occasionally run your ball
under very cold water—the "shock" of switching
the fleece from hot to cold increases the speed
with which it will felt. Continue to roll the ball
between your palms until it reaches its desired
smoothness and size. If felting time is slowing
down, use hotter water and/or more soap.

Multicolored Felt Balls
Follow felting instructions above until ball is
partially felted. Once the shape of the ball
is formed, choose contrasting color(s) (CC),
dampen in the soap and water, and place in the
desired position on the partially felted ball.
Using the felting needle, with a gentle stabbing
motion, secure the fleece into place. (Note:
Felting needles are very sharp and have a
barbed point; the barbed point helps to stick
the fleece together.) Continue stabbing until the
CC is tacked into place in desired shape,
then continue felting as above until the ball has
reached desired smoothness and size.

Finishing
Beaded Embellishment: Coat a short pin
with a bit of glue, then slip seed bead onto
pin and insert into felt ball in desired location.
Ornaments: Using 8–10" of leather threaded
onto yarn needle, insert needle up through one
or more felted balls, then back down through in
the opposite direction, leaving a $2\frac{1}{2}$" loop at the
top. Secure leather by knotting both ends at
the base of the ornament. Embellish as desired.
Garland: Thread leather onto yarn needle;
string felted balls onto leather, spacing them
approximately $2\frac{1}{2}$" apart; tie a knot on either
side of each ball to secure in place.

AMANDA BLAIR BROWN
Pompom Garland

Weave a magic web around your Christmas tree with these glittery, whimsical, and very original garlands made from knitted I-cords braided together and then dotted with playful pompoms. The cords can be made any length, and the pompoms are removable, making it easy to experiment until you find just the right way to mix and match them.

YARN
Classic Elite Waterspun (100% felted merino wool; 138 yards / 50 grams): 3 or 4 colors of choice, or as indicated below for each Garland
Note: 10 yards yarn will make approx 2 feet I-cord.
Classic Elite La Gran Mohair (76.5% mohair / 17.5% wool / 6% nylon; 90 yards / 42 grams): 1 ball makes approximately 8 solid-color pompoms; also used with gold cord for wrapping braids
Metallic cord (sold at craft/paper stores): 1 roll each thin gold and silver cord for wrapping braids and making shimmering pompoms
Shown in the following colors:
Note: Numbers beginning with 5 are for Waterspun; numbers beginning with 6 are for La Gran.
Pink Garland (opposite): #5068 madder (brick), #5019 India pink, #5089 Julia's pink (light pink), and #5087 bisque (tan); wrapped with #6519 cameo (light) pink and gold cord.
Green Garland (page 23): #5035 fern green (olive), #5074 pastoral green (yellowish green), #5036 celery (light green); wrapped with #6539 eucalyptus green and gold cord.

NEEDLES
Two double-pointed needles (dpn) size US 7 (4.5 mm) for I-cord

NOTIONS
10 large safety pins, yarn needle, 2 pieces cardboard, each 4" square for pompoms

GAUGE
Not crucial for this project

Garland

I-Cords
Using Waterspun, make 3 or 4 15-foot (or desired length) 4-stitch I-cords for each strand of garland (see Special Techniques, page 175). *Note: The finished garland will be slightly shorter than the length of each I-cord.*

Pompoms
Using La Gran and Waterspun, make 15 Pompoms, each approximately 4" in diameter, in colors desired (see Special Techniques, page 176). Mix and match yarn colors and fibers for interesting effects. Mix in gold and silver cord for extra shine.

Finishing
Tie 3 or 4 I-cords together at one end. With a safety pin, attach tied end to a stationary object. Loosely braid I-cords together, securing at 3-foot intervals with safety pins; tie I-cord ends together. *Note: Instructions for making a 4-strand braid appear on page 169.*

Wrap Garland: Cut 2 strands of La Gran and gold cord each 20 feet in length; holding one strand of each color together, tie ends to one end of the braid; loosely wrap strands around the braid, making a full wrap every 6"; tie strands to the other end of the braid. With remaining strands threaded onto yarn needle, tie ends to one end of the braid; loosely wrap strands around the braid in the opposite direction, making a full wrap every 6"; tie strands to opposite end of the braid. Remove safety pins.

Attach Pompoms: Attach 13 pompoms, evenly spaced, along the length of the garland by bringing pompom ends around each side of braid and knotting tightly; tie remaining 2 pompoms onto each end of garland. Trim pompom ties.

The yarns used for this jolly set of stockings come from La Lana Wools of Taos, New Mexico, where Sandy Cushman loves to visit at all times of the year. Here, she has tried to capture the subtle palette of the landscape in that part of the country in both color and texture—the hard-scrabble desert, the verdant mountains, and the sunshine that makes everything brighter and warmer, especially in winter. The vibrant, earthy colors she has chosen are repeated in the batik-print lining sewn inside each stocking, another reminder that holiday celebrations in many parts of the world—including much of the United States—are often anything but red and green.

FINISHED MEASUREMENTS
Approximately 20 (22, 24, 26, 28)" long

YARN
Yarn 1: La Lana Knitting Worsted (100% wool; 200 yards / 4 ounces): grape (A), apple green (B), and burgundy (C)
Yarn 2: La Lana Forever Random Blends (wool / mohair blends; 80 yards / 2 ounces): Chaco Canyon (D), yellow brick road (E), faerie queen (F), and primavera (G)
Note: Each Stocking will use 2½ –3 skeins yarn, depending on the size of Stocking; mix and match colors as desired, or work as shown.

NEEDLES
One 16" circular needle size US 9 (5.5 mm)
One set of five 6" double-pointed needles (dpn) size US 9 (5.5 mm)
One set of five 8" double-pointed needles size US 9 (5.5 mm)
Change needle size if necessary to obtain correct gauge.

Stocking styles shown (left to right): 2, 4, 1

NOTIONS
45" wide lining fabric: ½ yard for Stockings 1 and 2; ¾ yard for Stockings 3 and 4; ⅝ yard for Stocking 5; 5 pieces ¾ yard ribbon, each 12" long, for hanger loops; waste yarn

GAUGE
Approximately 17½ sts and 17½ rows = 4" (10 cm) in Slip stitch pattern from Chart using Yarns 1 and 2
17 sts and 22 rows = 4" (10 cm) in Stockinette stitch (St st) using Yarn 1
Note: Gauge within stocking is variable due to character of yarn and Stitch patterns.

Shown in the following colors/sizes:
Stocking 1: 20" long in Slip st pattern, using B and G for toe, foot, and leg; A and F for Ribbed Top and Heel.
Stocking 2: 22" long in Stripe pattern, using C, F and G for toe, foot, and leg; A for ribbed Top and Heel.
Stocking 3: 24" long in Slip st pattern, using A and E for toe, foot, and leg; C for ribbed Top and Heel.
Stocking 4: 26" long in Stripe pattern, using B and A for toe, foot, and leg; F for ribbed Top and Heel.
Stocking 5: 28" long in Slip st pattern, using D and C for toe, foot, and leg; A and B for ribbed Top and Heel.

NOTES
✳ These stockings are knit from the toe up to the Ribbed Top, with only a short pause to insert waste yarn where the future heel will be. For ease in working, change from dpn to circ needle when sufficient sts have been increased.
✳ When working Slip st pattern, strand yarn loosely behind slipped sts to prevent fabric from puckering.

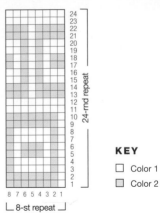

KEY

☐ Color 1

☐ Color 2

⌐ 8-st repeat ⌐

❋ **Slip Stitch Pattern**

(multiple of 8 sts; 24-rnd repeat)

Note: See Chart for color placement.

Rnds 1 and 2: * Slip 1, k7; repeat from *
around.

Rnds 3 and 4: * K1, slip 1, k5, slip 1; repeat
from * around.

Rnds 5 and 6: * Slip 1, k1, slip 1, k3, slip 1,
k1; repeat from * around.

Rnds 7 and 8: Repeat Rnds 3 and 4.

Rnds 9 and 10: Repeat Rnds 1 and 2.

Rnds 11 and 12: Knit.

Rnds 13 and 14: K4, * slip 1, K7; repeat to
last 4 sts, slip 1, k3.

Rnds 15 and 16: K3, * slip 1, k1, slip 1, k5;
repeat to last 5 sts, slip 1, k1, slip 1, k2.

Rnds 17 and 18: K2, * slip 1, k1, slip 1, k1,
slip 1, k3; repeat to last 6 sts, slip 1, k1, slip
1, k1, slip 1, k1.

Rnds 19 and 20: Repeat Rnds 15 and 16.

Rnds 21 and 22: Repeat Rnds 13 and 14.

Rnds 23 and 24: Knit.

Repeat Rnds 1–24 for Slip st pattern.

❋ **Make Bobble** (mb)

Knit in [front, back, front] of next st to increase to 3 sts, turn; p3, turn; pass first st
over second st, pass second st over third st
to decrease to one st.

❋ **Bobble BO**

All Stockings: K1, * mb, pass first st over
bobble to BO 1 st, knit bobble st (pulling
to tighten bobble); k1, pass bobble st over
knit st, [p1, pass last st over st] 2 times, k1,
pass last st over st; rep from * around.

General Instructions (All Stockings)

Toe Flap

Using 2 dpns and B (C, E, B, D), CO 6 (6, 6, 6, 8)
sts; begin St st. Work even for 11 (11, 11, 13, 15)
rows; DO NOT TURN. Rotate work to pick up
and knit 8 (8, 8, 10, 12) sts along side with
Needle 2; rotate to pick up and knit 6 (6, 6, 6, 8)
sts across bottom (CO edge) with Needle 3;
rotate to pick up and knit 8 (8, 8, 10, 12) sts
along other side with Needle 4; then k2 (2, 2,
2, 3) sts from Needle 1 with Needle 4.
Join for working in the rnd.

Knit 1 rnd, distributing sts evenly on four
needles—7 (7, 7, 8, 10) sts on each needle;
place marker (pm) for beginning of rnd —
28 (28, 28, 32, 40) sts.

Toe

Rnd 1—Increase rnd: * K1, M1, knit to end of
Needle 1; knit to 2 sts from end of Needle 2,
M1, k1; repeat from * for Needles 3 and 4.
Rnd 2: Knit even.

Repeat Rnds 1 and 2 until there are 12 (13, 14,
15, 16) sts on each needle—48 (52, 56, 60, 64)
sts total.

SLIP STITCH STOCKINGS

Stockings 1 (3, 5)

Foot: Join G (E, C); begin Slip st pattern and
Chart. Repeating Rnds 1–24 of stitch pattern,
work 35 (47, 59) rnds, ending Rnd 11 (23, 11)
of stitch pattern.

Mark for Heel: Using waste yarn, knit across
Needles 1 and 2, turn; purl across Needles 2
and 1.

Leg: Continuing as established, work Rnd(s)
12–24 (24, 12–24) of Slip st pattern once,
then repeat Rnds 1–24 of Chart 2 (3, 3) times—
61 (73, 85) rnds.

Stocking styles shown
(left to right): 5, 3

STRIPED STOCKINGS

Stocking 2: 3-Color Stripe Sequence
Begin St st.
Foot: Join F; work 3-color Stripe sequence
[2 rnds F, 2 rnds G, 2 rnds C] 6 times, ending last repeat with 1 rnd C—35 rnds.
Mark for Heel: Using waste yarn, knit across Needles 1 and 2, turn; purl across Needles 2 and 1.
Leg: Beginning with 1 rnd C, repeat 3-color Stripe sequence 8 more times—49 rnds.

Stocking 4: 2-Color Stripe Sequence
Begin St st.
Foot: Join A; work 2-color Stripe sequence
[2 rnds A, 2 rnds B] 11 times, ending last repeat with 1 rnd B—43 rnds.
Mark for Heel: Using waste yarn, knit across Needles 1 and 2, turn; purl across Needles 2 and 1.
Leg: Beginning with 1 rnd B, repeat 2-color Stripe sequence 17 more times—69 rnds.

ALL STOCKINGS
Ribbed Top
Join A (A, C, F, A); knit 1 rnd even.
Increase Rnd: * K1, M1, k1, p2; repeat from * around—60 (65, 70, 75, 80) sts.
Ribbing: Work in k3, p2 rib as established until Ribbed Top measures 2½", using colors as follows:
Stocking 1: Join F; alternate 2 rnds A, 2 rnds F for length.
Stockings 2, 3, and 4: Cont with color established.
Stocking 5: Join E; alternate 2 rnds A, 2 rnds E for length.
BO all sts using Bobble BO.

Heel
Carefully remove waste yarn and place sts from top and bottom of heel opening on 2 needles.
Pick up an extra st at the end of each needle—52 (56, 60, 64, 68) sts total. Divide sts evenly onto 4 needles; join A (A, C, F, A).
Rnd 1—Decrease Rnd: * K1, k2tog, knit to end of Needle 1; knit to last 3 sts on Needle 2, ssk, k1; repeat from * for Needles 3 and 4.
Rnd 2: Knit even.
Working Heel in same color(s) as for Ribbed Top, repeat Rnds 1 and 2 until there are 4 (4, 4, 5, 5) sts remaining on each needle.
Slip sts from Needle 2 onto Needle 1 and sts from Needle 3 onto Needle 4; graft sts together using Kitchener st (see Special Techniques, page 176). Weave in ends.

Lining
Fold lining fabric in half with RS's together. Place completed Stocking (with Ribbed Top folded down as in photo) on fabric and carefully trace around Stocking. Cut fabric along tracing, cutting ½" larger than tracing along top edge of Stocking. Using ½" seam allowance, with RS's together, sew lining, leaving top open. Fold top edge ½" down to WS and press. Fold one 12" long piece of ribbon in half. Turn lining RS out and stitch lining to inside top edge of Stocking, securing ribbon in between center back of Stocking and lining. Tack lining to Heel and Toe.

Knitting with wire and beads can be a spiritual experience, says designer Annie Modesitt. The feeling of slipping the beads along the wire as well as the color, texture, and brightness of this medium all invite introspection and provide sensations not common to ordinary knitting. Particularly unusual is the experience of seeing individual knit stitches backlit by soft candlelight, which is what you'll enjoy after knitting these unique votive sleeves. For a menorah, knit eight in one height and one slightly larger, then arrange them in a line or semicircle. Or, if you wish, use them in different numbers and arrangements to add a unique touch to any celebration of light.

FINISHED MEASUREMENTS
$2\frac{1}{2}$ (3)" high by the circumference of votive holder

MATERIALS
Artistic Wire (24 gauge): 5 yards for each Votive Sleeve (45 yards total for pieces as shown), in color gunmetal; 140 (200) sizes 6–8 glass beads for each Votive Sleeve (1,320 beads for pieces as shown), in various colors

NEEDLES
One pair straight aluminum needles size US 8 (5 mm)

NOTIONS
Smooth needle-nose pliers

GAUGE
Not essential

Votive Sleeve

Note: This sleeve is designed to go around the holder, NOT around the actual candle. Instructions below will create a Votive Sleeve that is $2\frac{1}{2}$ (3)" high and as big around as you desire, to fit your votive candle holder.

Before You Begin: String 140 (200) beads onto a 5-yard piece of wire in a random fashion. Using a single strand of beaded wire and a very loose Backward Loop CO method (see Special Techniques, page 174), CO 8 (10) sts as follows: CO 1 st, [slip 1 bead to needle, CO 1 st] 7 (9) times.

Set-up Row: P1, [slip 1 bead to needle, p1] 7 (9) times.

Row 1 (RS): K1, [slip 1 bead to needle, k1] 7 (9) times.

Row 2: P1, [slip 1 bead to needle, p1] 7 (9) times.

Rows 3 and 4: Repeat Rows 1 and 2.

Note: For a votive candle holder with straight sides, omit Rows 5 and 6. For a shaped votive candle holder, work Short Rows as follows:

Row 5: [K1, slip 1 bead to needle] 4 (5) times, wrap and turn (wrp-t).

Row 6: P1, [sl 1 bead to needle, p1] 3 (4) times.

Repeat Rows 1–4 < Rows 1–6 >, "blocking" piece as you go by pulling and stretching wire fabric until the sts look even. Continue working until the edge < shorter edge > is long enough to reach around the candle holder—16 rows shown in photo; end with a WS row. Cut wire, leaving an 8 (10)" tail.

Finishing

Join CO and final row with the tail, weaving it between CO edge and live sts, one by one, working to the bottom of the sleeve.

Push the wire ends from the front to the back of the work. Using needle-nose pliers, twist the wires together, then coil them into a tight circle. Press this firmly (with the broader part of the pliers) into the inner edge of the Votive sleeve.

VÉRONIK AVERY
Lace Photo Mats

During holiday celebrations families and friends inevitably reminisce about the events of the year just past. These knitted-lace photograph mats offer a beautiful way to preserve those special memories.

FINISHED MEASUREMENTS
Willow Leaf (opposite, right): 8" by 10"
Lace Cable: 11" by 14"

YARN
Lana Gatto Wool Gatto from Needful Yarns (100% wool; 181 yd / 50 grams): #20439 silver gray (MC)
Note: Quantities will vary, depending on size of mat, but 1 ball is usually sufficient for 2 to 3 mats.

NEEDLES
One pair straight needles size US 2 (2.75 mm)
Change needle size if necessary to obtain correct gauge.

NOTIONS
Yarn needle, cable needle (cn), stitch holders, contrasting waste yarn

GAUGE
24 sts and 48 rows = 4" (10 cm) in Garter stitch

NOTES
⁂ **Yarn-Over Short Rows**
  Corners of Lace Cable Mat
  (RS) Step 1: Work as indicated across row, turn; DO NOT wrap next st.
  (WS) Step 2: Begin row with yo (see Special Techniques, page 178), then work as indicated to end.
  (RS) Step 3: Close gap where indicated by knitting the yo from the previous row together with the next stitch.

Willow Leaf Mat

Using waste yarn, CO 12 sts; knit 1 row. Break waste yarn. Join MC; purl 1 (WS) row.
Note: The strip will be composed of 4 segments, separated by 3 sections of waste yarn.

* First Width
Begin Willow Leaf pattern from Chart, Row 1.
Repeat Rows 1–8 until piece measures approximately 5" from the beginning, or 3" less than inner width of frame, ending Row 8 of stitch pattern.

Establish Corner
Without breaking MC, knit 2 rows using waste yarn; break waste yarn.

First Length
Using MC, knit 1 row. Begin Willow Leaf pattern from Chart, Row 1.
Work as for First Width until piece measures approximately 7" from waste yarn corner, or 3" less than inner length of frame; establish corner using waste yarn.

Second Width and Length
Repeat from * once, ending second length with Row 8 of stitch pattern; DO NOT work 2 rows waste yarn.

First Corner
(RS) Continuing with 12 sts of Second Length, k12; with RS facing, taking care not to twist frame, pick up and knit 12 sts from CO row—24 sts.
Row 1 (WS): K2tog, k10, place marker (pm), k10, ssk.
Row 2: Knit across to 2 sts before marker, ssk, slip marker (sm), k2tog, knit to end.
Row 3: Knit.
Repeat Rows 2 and 3 until 2 sts remain.
Cut yarn and pull through remaining sts.

Remaining Corners
With RS facing and garter edge at right, pick up and knit 12 sts on each side of waste yarn at next corner—24 sts; remove waste yarn. Work remaining 3 corners as for First Corner, beginning with Row 1.

Finishing
Weave in ends. Pin mat to desired dimensions (a template can be made from a tracing of the frame's backing). Spray or steam and let dry. Once dry, attach mat to a piece of light cardboard by tacking lightly with hot glue. Slip image in through the front opening, and frame as usual.

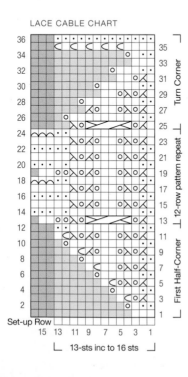

8
6
4
2

7
5
3
1

11 9 7 5 3 1

⌐ 12-st repeat ⌐

✳ Willow Leaf Pattern

(Multiple of 12 sts; 8-row repeat) (See Chart)
Row 1 (RS): *Yo, k1, yo, k2, [k2tog] twice,
k2, yo, k2tog, k1; repeat from * across.
Row 2 and all WS rows: *K2, p10; repeat
from * across.
Row 3: *Yo, k3, yo, k1, [k2tog] twice, k1, yo,
k2tog, k1; repeat from * across.
Row 5: *Yo, k5, yo, [k2tog] twice, yo, k2tog,
k1; repeat from * across.
Row 7: *Yo, k3, k2tog, k2, [yo, k2tog] twice,
k1; repeat from * across.
Row 8: *K2, p10; repeat from * across.
Repeat Rows 1-8 for Willow Leaf pattern.

LACE CABLE CHART

36
34
32
30
28
26
24
22
20
18
16
14
12
10
8
6
4
2
Set-up Row

35
33
31
29
27
25
23
21
19
17
15
13
11
9
7
5
3
1

Turn Corner

12-row pattern repeat

First Half-Corner

15 13 11 9 7 5 3 1

⌐ 13-sts inc to 16 sts ⌐

✳ Lace Cable Pattern

(Multiple of 13 sts, inc to 16 sts;
12-row repeat) (See Chart)
Row 13: K1, k2tog, yo, 3/3 RC, yo, ssk,
[yo] twice, k2—15 sts.
Rows 14 and 20: K2, [k1, p1, k1] into
double yo from previous row, purl across to
last 2 sts, k2—16 sts.
Rows 15, 17, 21, and 23: K1, k2tog, yo,
ssk, yo, k2, yo, k2tog, yo, ssk, k5.
Rows 16 and 22: K5, purl across to last
2 sts, k2.
Row 18: BO 3, k2, purl across to last 2 sts,
k2—13 sts.
Row 19: K1, k2tog, yo, ssk, yo, k2, yo,
k2tog, yo, ssk, [yo] twice, k2—15 sts.
Row 24: Repeat Row 18.
Repeat Rows 13–24 for Lace
Cable pattern.

Turn Corner of Lace Cable Pattern

Short Rows (Multiple of 13 sts; 12 rows)
Row 25: K1, k2tog, yo, 3/3 RC, yo,
ssk, turn.
Rows 26, 28, 30, 32 and 34: Yo, purl across
to last 2 sts, k2.
Row 27: K1, k2tog, yo, ssk, yo, k2, yo,
k2tog, turn.
Row 29: K1, k2tog, yo, ssk, yo, k2, turn.
Row 31: K1, k2tog, yo, k2, turn.
Row 33: K3, turn.
Row 35: Knit across, closing gaps.
Row 36: Knit.

KEY

☐ Knit on RS, purl on WS.

⊡ Purl on RS, knit on WS.

◙ Yo

⧄ K2tog

⧅ Ssk

⧄ Short Rows—Close gap:
   Knit the yo from the previous row
   together with the next st as in K2tog.

☐ Short Rows: Stitch left unworked.

▨ No stitch

⬛ Bind off 1 stitch.

⨯ **3/3 RC**: Slip 3 sts to cn, hold to back,
   k3, k3 from cn.

CREATING—AND PRESERVING—HOLIDAY MEMORIES

We all grow up with certain holiday traditions and then create some of our own as adults. Here are a few ideas for knitting-related traditions you might want to try out in your home.

Frame holiday photos using the Lace Photo Mats (pattern starts on page 22).

Knit the same type of garment for each family member. For example, you could start with the Candy Cane Hats on page 64. Knit a new colorway of the same hat or a completely different style of hat each year.

Knit at least one item to donate to charity every December. Check out local charities or the list of national charities on page 120.

Host a series of *Handknit Holidays* **parties.** Invite knitting friends and family members to your home on a regular basis (once a month throughout the year or maybe just once in the fall—whatever suits your lifestyle). Adding this social element to holiday-knitting plans may help everyone to finish their projects on time. For more holiday-knitting strategies, see page 165.

Gather with the family for a night of ornament-making. Check out the pattern for Knitted and Felted Ornaments on page 10. Also consider making fancy pompoms for the tree like those featured on the Pompom Garland on page 14. Choose a different type of wooly ornament to make each year.

Get together with your knitting group for a holiday bash. Plan on working on a different group project each year. To start, check out the Community Afghan on page 94.

Schedule at least a few hours (or days) of peaceful knitting before your calendar gets too full of holiday commitments. Be sure to write the dates on the calendar so you won't forget or let chores take precedence.

❊ **First Half-Corner of Lace Cable Pattern**
Short Rows (Multiple of 13 sts; 12-rows)
(Also see Chart, Rows 1–12)
Row 1 (RS): K3, turn.
Rows 2, 4, 6, 8, and 10: Yo, purl to last 2 sts, k2.
Row 3: K1, k2tog, yo, close gap, k1, turn.
Row 5: K1, k2tog, yo, ssk, yo, close gap, k1, turn.
Row 7: K1, k2tog, yo, ssk, yo, k2, close gap, k1, turn.
Row 9: K1, k2tog, yo, ssk, yo, k2, yo, k2tog, close gap, k1, turn.
Row 11: K1, k2tog, yo, ssk, yo, k2, yo, k2tog, yo, ssk, close gap, k1.
Row 12 (WS): K2, purl to last 2 sts, k2.
These 12 rows complete First Half-Corner— 13 sts.

Lace Cable Mat

Using waste yarn and Provisional CO method (see Special Techniques, page 176), CO 13 sts. Break waste yarn.
Join MC; knit 1 (WS) row.
First Half-Corner
Begin Lace Cable pattern from Chart, Row 1; work Rows 1–12 once. Pm for beginning of side.
✽ **Side—Width**
Work Rows 13 –24, then repeat these Rows only until piece measures 9½" from marker, or 1½" less than inner width of frame.
Turn Corner
Work Rows 25–36 once. Complete Corner by working Rows 1–12 once; pm.
Side—Length
Work as for Side Width until piece measures 12½" from marker, or 1½" less than inner length of frame. Turn Corner by working Rows 25–36 once, then Rows 1–12 once; pm.
Remaining 2 Sides
Repeat from ✽, turning corners as before.

Finishing
Break yarn, leaving a 12" tail. Remove waste yarn from CO row; place sts on a second needle. With WS facing, and yarn threaded on a yarn needle, graft last row to CO row using Kitchener st (see Special Techniques, page 176). Weave in loose ends.
Block as for Willow Leaf Mat.

Hannah's Tablecloth

Annie Modesitt's grandmother once knitted a tablecloth that became a treasured family heirloom, and it inspired Annie to make one to pass on to her own daughter. But knitting an entire tablecloth can seem insurmountable, especially when a holiday deadline is looming. Annie's clever, timesaving solution utilizes linen napkins, knitted together in a lace pattern and edged with linen yarn.

FINISHED MEASUREMENTS
77" long by 52" wide

YARN
Louet Euroflax Sportweight Linen (100% linen; 135 yards / 50 grams): 6 skeins pure white

NEEDLES
Two 36" circular (circ) needles size US 4 (3.5 mm)
Change needle size if necessary to obtain correct gauge.

NOTIONS
Six 21" square linen napkins, stitch holders, stitch markers, darning needles, steam iron, and ironing board

GAUGE
16 sts and 26 rows = 4" (10 cm) in Stockinette stitch (St st)

NOTES
✳ **Double Centered Decrease** (dcd)
Slip 2 sts as if to k2tog to right-hand needle, k1, pass 2 slipped sts over knit st.

Tablecloth

Prepare Napkins
Using a single strand of yarn, whipstitch around the edges of each napkin, making 42 sts along each edge and 1 st on each corner—a total of 172 sts around each napkin.

Lace Edging
Napkin Side 1: Knit the first corner st on a napkin, place marker (pm), [yo, knit next whipstitch] 42 times, yo, pm—86 sts.
Napkin Sides 2, 3, and 4: Repeat Side 1—344 sts.
Continue working in the rnd; begin Lace patterns, slipping markers as you come to them; work the corner sts in Chart B, the side sts in Chart A as follows:
Rnd 1: * [Yo, k1, yo] in corner st [Rnd 1, Chart B]; k85 [Rnd 1, Chart A]; repeat from * around.
Rnd 2: * [Yo, k3, yo] in corner st [Rnd 2, chart B], k85 [Rnd 2, Chart A]; repeat from * around.
Continue from Charts as established until Rnd 12 has been completed, ending Rnds 9–12 as indicated on Chart.
* Slip 13 corner sts onto a strand of waste yarn or stitch holder, slip 85 side sts onto separate strand of waste yarn or stitch holder; repeat from * around. Set napkin aside.
Work Lace edging on remaining 5 napkins.

Finishing

Assemble Napkins (see Diagram)

Sides: Slip 85 sts from one napkin side holder onto one circ needle; slip 85 sts from a second napkin onto the other circ needle. Arrange napkins so right sides are facing up and sts that are on circ needles are next to each other. Using Kitchener st (see Special Techniques, page 176), graft the two sides of the first 2 napkins together, matching motifs. Leave the corner stitches on holders. Attach 3 napkins together to make one strip, then attach the remaining 3 for a second strip. Lay these two long pieces side by side and, working on one 85-st section at a time, graft the sides together to form a piece 3 napkins long by 2 napkins wide.

Center Circles: Working on one of the two areas where four napkins come together, using a triple strand of linen yarn, thread 13 sts from each of the 4 corners together—a total of 52 sts. Tie off triple strand, leaving a 1" circle. Repeat with remaining center corner area.

chart a
SIDE STITCHES

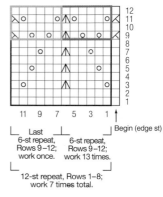

11 9 7 5 3 1 ↑

Last
6-st repeat,
Rows 9–12;
work once.

6-st repeat,
Rows 9–12;
work 13 times.

Begin (edge st)

12-st repeat, Rows 1–8;
work 7 times total.

chart b
CORNER STITCHES

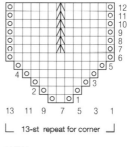

13 11 9 7 5 3 1

13-st repeat for corner

KEY

☐	Knit on RS, purl on WS	☒	Ssk
☉	Yo	☒	Dcd
☒	K2tog		

hannah's tablecloth assembly

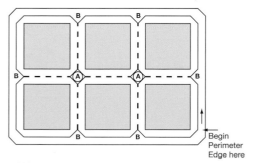

Begin
Perimeter
Edge here

KEY

A Center circles

B Perimeter decrease, Rnd 1

– – Join sides using Kitchener st

Edging

Slip all stitches, including corner stitches, from the outer edges of the tablecloth onto one circ needle—1058 sts. (Alternatively, you may want to place half the sts on a second circ needle to make working the edging easier.)

Rnd 1: Beginning at first set of side sts along the shorter edge of the tablecloth, * k85 across first side section to where two 13-st corners meet; [slip 6 sts, k1, pass slipped sts over knit st, k13, pass next 6 sts over last knit st—14 sts rem at corners]; k85, k13 corner sts, k85, repeat [ ], k85 sts, repeat [ ], k85, k13 corner sts.
Repeat from * around—986 sts remain.

Rnd 2: Purl.

Rnds 3 and 4: Knit.

Rnd 5: * P2tog, yo; repeat from * around to create Fold line.

Rnds 6 and 7: Knit.

Bind off all sts loosely.

Note: Because linen does not felt, it is necessary to knot ends of yarn together. These ends can be separated into thinner strands and woven in, but unless the joins are knotted, the fabric may come apart with repeated washings. After the linen fabric is knit, it can be treated the same as the linen napkin when washing, drying, and ironing the finished tablecloth.

Hem

Steam-press lace edging around circumference. Fold hem at Row 5, creating a picot edge; hand-stitch bound-off edge to WS of work, being careful not to pull the hem too tightly. Dampen the entire tablecloth, then steam-press with a very hot iron. Start by steam-press/blocking the knit lace sections, then press the linen napkin areas of the tablecloth.

Gina Wilde has been dressing animals since she was small—though she no longer puts blue eye shadow on her Siamese cat, or a black velvet bikini on her English bull terrier, as she did as a child. Instead, she's called upon that innocent fascination with animals to create these fanciful feline and canine friends, bold and adorable gifts that children can dress and undress all they please.

FINISHED MEASUREMENTS
Approximately 26" tall

YARN
Alchemy Lone Star (55% mohair / 45% merino); 135 yards / 100 grams: 3 skeins each in #81f house finch (A) and #31e olive branch (B).
2 skeins each in #49s punky (C) and #59s rainforest (D).
Alchemy Synchronicity (50% silk / 50% wool; 110 yards / 50 grams): 1 skein each in #48a passion flower (E), #82w Janboy's sapphire (F).
Odd scraps of yarn for embroidering facial features (both); hair and collar (cat); bandana detail (dog).
Shown in the following colors:
Kitty (A); Pup (B); Skirt (C); Blouse (E); Overalls (D); Bandana (F)

NEEDLES
One pair straight needles size US 8 (5 mm)
One 16" circular (circ) needle size US 8 (5 mm)
Two double-pointed needles (dpn) size US 8 (5 mm)
Change needle size if necessary to obtain correct gauge.

NOTIONS
Yarn needle, stitch holders, fiberfill or other stuffing (for bodies), embroidery needle

GAUGE
18 sts and 22 rows = 4" (10 cm) in Stockinette stitch (St st) using Reservoir
20 sts and 26 rows = 4" (10 cm) in St st using Synchronicity

Kitty (Pup) Body

Arm (make 2)
Using A (B), CO 10 sts.
Rows 1 and 3: Purl.
Row 2 (RS): K1, * M1, k1; repeat from * to end—19 sts.
Row 4: K8, [M1, k1] 3 times, k8—22 sts.
Rows 5–15: Work even in St st.
Row 16: * K2tog, k7, skp; repeat from * once—18 sts remain.
Row 17: Purl.
Row 18: K1, M1, knit across to last st, M1, k1—20 sts.
Rows 19–25: Work even in St st.
Rows 26–57: Repeat Rows 18–25; after Row 50—28 sts.
Rows 58–70: Work even in St st.
BO all sts loosely; sew seams.

Leg (make 2)
Using A (B), CO 24 sts.
Rows 1 and 3: Purl.
Row 2 (RS): K1, * k1-f/b; repeat from * to last st, k1—46 sts.
Row 4: [K1, M1] twice, k18, [M1, k1] 5 times, k18, [M1, k1] twice—54 sts.
Rows 5–11: Work even in St st.
Row 12: K24, k2tog, k1, skp, k25—52 sts remain.
Rows 13, 15, and 17: Purl.
Row 14: K23, k2tog, k1, skp, k24—50 sts remain.
Row 16: K22, k2tog, k1, skp, k23—48 sts remain.
Row 18: K14, BO next 20 sts, knit to end—28 sts remain.
Row 19: P14, close gap over BO sts, p14—28 sts.
Rows 20–79: Work even in St st.
BO all sts loosely; sew leg and foot seam.

Body and Head

Using A (B), CO 56 sts.

Shape Body: Rows 1, 3, 5, 7, and 9: Purl.

Row 2 (RS): K13, [M1, k1] 3 times, k12, M1, k13, [M1, k1] 3 times, k12—63 sts.

Row 4: K31, M1, k1, M1, k31—65 sts.

Row 6: K31, M1, k3, M1, k31—67 sts.

Row 8: K31, M1, k5, M1, k31—69 sts.

Rows 10–25: Work even in St st.

Row 26: K13, k2tog, k1, skp, k33, k2tog, k1, skp, k13—65 sts remain.

Rows 27–31: Work even in St st.

Row 32: K12, k2tog, k1, skp, k31, k2tog, k1, skp, k12—61 sts remain.

Rows 33–37: Work even in St st.

Row 38: K11, k2tog, k1, skp, k29, k2tog, k1, skp, k11—57.

Rows 39–43: Work even in St st.

Row 44: K10, k2tog, k1, skp, k11, skp, k1, k2tog, k11, k2tog, k1, skp, k10—51 sts remain.

Rows 45, 47, and 49: Purl.

Row 46: K23, skp, k1, k2tog, k23— 49 sts remain.

Row 48: K22, skp, k1, k2tog, k22— 47 sts remain.

Row 50: K9, k2tog, k1, skp, k7, skp, k1, k2tog, k7, k2tog, k1, skp, k9—41 sts remain for Head.

Row 51: Purl.

Shape Head: Row 52: K20, M1, k1, M1, k20— 43 sts.

Rows 53–57: Work even in St st.

Row 58: K1, [M1, k20, M1, k1] twice—47 sts.

Rows 59–61: Work even in St st.

Row 62: K23, M1, k1, M1, k23—49 sts.

Row 63: P24, M1, p1, M1, p24—51 sts.

Row 64: K1, [M1, k24, M1, k1] twice—55 sts.

Row 65: P27, M1, p1, M1, p27—57 sts.

Rows 66–67: Work even in St st.

Row 68: K1, [skp, k23, k2tog, k1] twice— 53 sts remain.

Rows 69–71: Work even in St st.

Row 72: K1, [skp, k21, k2tog, k1] twice— 49 sts remain.

Rows 73, 75, 77, 79, and 81: Purl.

Row 74: K1, skp, k5, skp, k29, k2tog, k5, k2tog, k1—45 sts remain.

Row 76: K1, [skp, k17, k2tog, k1] twice— 41 sts remain.

Row 78: K1, skp, k3, skp, k25, k2tog, k3, k2tog, k1—37 sts remain.

Row 80: K1, [skp, k13, k2tog, k1] twice— 33 sts remain.

Row 82: [K1, skp] twice, k8, k2tog, k1, skp, k8 [k2tog, k1] twice—27 sts remain.

Row 83: Purl.

BO all sts loosely.

Kitty Ears

Outer Ear (make 2)

Using A, CO 9 sts.

Rows 1–4: Work even in St st.

Row 5: Decrease 1 st each side—7 sts remain.

Rows 6 and 7: Work even in St st.

Rows 8–13: Repeat Rows 5–7 twice—
3 sts remain.

Row 14: Work 3 sts together—1 st remains.
Fasten off.

Inner Ear (make 2)

Using scrap yarn, CO 7 sts.

Rows 1–3: Work even in St st.

Row 4: Decrease 1 st each side—5 sts remain.

Rows 5 and 6: Work even in St st.

Row 7: Repeat Row 4—3 sts remain.

Row 8: Work 3 sts together—1 st remains.
Fasten off.

With WS facing (RS's held together),
sew inner ear to outer ear. Turn RS out
and sew bottom seam.

Pup Ears

Outer Ear (make 2)

Using B, * CO 2 sts; begin St st.

(WS) Purl 1 row.

Shape Ear: (RS) Increase 1 st each side this
row, then every other row 6 times—16 sts.
Work even for 5 rows.

Decrease 1 st each side this row, then every
4 rows 2 times—10 sts remain.

Work 1 row even; pm each side this row. *
Decrease 1 st at end of this row, then every
other row 3 times—6 sts remain.

Work 1 row even; BO all sts.

Inner Ear (make 2)

Using scrap yarn, work from * to * of outer Ear.
Next Row: Decreasing 1 st at each side, BO all
sts. Sew pieces together as for Kitty Ears.

Kitty Tail

Using A, CO 15 sts; begin St st. Work even
until piece measures 9" from beginning, ending
with a WS row.

Shape Tail: Decrease 1 st each side this row,
then every 4th row until 7 sts remain.
BO all sts loosely; sew seam, including tip of tail.

Kitty Hair

*Note: The number of sts needed will depend on
the gauge of the yarn being used.*

Using scrap yarn, CO and work a Garter st rectangle approximately 1" by 5"; BO all sts loosely.

Finishing

*Stuffing Note: Use small pieces (about
an inch or two in size) as the smaller pieces
will blend together nicely, preventing a
lumpy appearance.*

Stuff Legs: Be sure foot is firmly filled; as you
move up the Leg with stuffing, ease the amount
as you draw near the top. This will make for
easier sewing together, as well as a finished
piece that sits cooperatively. Sew top of
Leg closed.

Stuff Arms: Fill hands firmly, and ease amount
of stuffing as for Legs toward the top of the
Arm. Sew top of Arm closed.

Stuff Body: Join Body and Head at back seam.
Stuff this piece, using the opening at the lower
edge of the Body; be sure to stuff face with
attention to shaping—fill out the Nose, ease a
bit through the Neck, etc.

Assemble Kitty/Pup: Insert top of Legs at
lower edge of Body; sew in place. Sew Arms in
place. Fold Ears in half lengthwise; sew in place.
Center Hair on top of Head, between Ears, and
sew in place.

If desired, make a French knot for belly button.

Embroider Face: The face is the personality of
your creation, so plan on devoting some time to
embroidering it—this isn't a rush job. Look at
the photo for ideas.

Be sure to make simple, clear stitches. If you
don't get exactly the look you desire in your first
attempt at embroidering, carefully remove the
stitches and try again. Be sure to give the open
eye of the cat a dark pupil, a definitive feature
that makes the cat come alive.

Clothing and Accessories

Holiday Collar

Using scrap yarn and dpn, CO 7 sts; begin
I-cord (see Special Techniques, page 175).
Work Collar to length desired (it should fit snugly
around Kitty's neck); BO all sts.

Berries

Using scrap yarn and dpn, CO 3 sts;
begin I-cord.
Work until piece measures $\frac{1}{2}$" from the beginning; do not BO. Join live sts to CO end, rolling into a ball.

Leaves

Using scrap yarn, CO 2 sts.
Row 1: Purl.
Row 2: K1-f/b of first and last st—4 sts.
Rows 3 and 4: Repeat Rows 1 and 2—6 sts.
Row 5: Purl.
Row 6: Ssk, knit across to last 2 sts, k2tog—
4 sts remain.
Rows 7 and 8: Repeat Rows 5 and 6—
2 sts remain.
Row 9: P2tog; fasten off.
Sew berries and leaves in place, and fasten
Collar at Back of neck.

Skirt

Using C and circular needle, CO 140 sts.
Join for working in the round, being careful not
to twist sts; place marker (pm) for beginning
of rnd. Begin Garter st.
Work even for 6 rnds in Garter st (purl 1 rnd,
knit 1 rnd). Change to St st; work even for 7".
Shape Skirt: * K2tog; repeat from * around—
70 sts remain.
Work even for 6 rnds in Garter st; BO remaining
sts loosely.
Straps (make 2): Using C, CO 40 sts. Knit even
for 2 rows; BO all sts loosely.
Weave in ends. Sew Straps to Skirt, adjusting
length as necessary to fit Kitty.

Blouse
Front

Using E, CO 40 sts; begin Seed st.
(RS) Work even for 2 rows, ending with a
WS row.
(RS) Change to St st; work even for 6 rows,
pm at each end of last (WS) row.
Work even for 16 more rows, ending with a
WS row.

Left Front/Back

Shape Shoulders and Neck: (RS) K9, turn.
Continuing in St st, working on these 9 sts only,
work even for 10 rows for shoulder strap; place
sts on holder.

Right Front/Back

(RS) Rejoin yarn at neck edge; BO next 22 sts
for neck, knit to end—9 sts remain. Work as
for left Front/Back for 10 rows; do not place
sts on holder.

Back

(WS) P9; CO 22 sts for Back neck; purl across
sts on holder for left Front—40 sts.
Continuing in St st, work even for 16 rows; pm
at each end of last (WS) row.
Work even for 6 rows. Change to Seed st; work
even for 2 rows. BO all sts loosely in pattern.

Sleeves

With RS facing, pick up and knit 46 sts between
markers. Begin Seed st; work even for 2 rows.
BO all sts loosely in pattern. Sew side and
sleeve seams.

Finishing

Neckband: With RS facing, pick up and knit
65 sts evenly around neck opening. Join for
working in the rnd; pm for beginning of rnd.
Begin Seed st; work 2 rnds even. BO all sts
loosely in pattern.

Overalls
Right Leg

Using D, * CO 40 sts; begin Garter st.
Work even for 6 rows.
Change to St st; work even for 6 rows.
Shape Leg: Increase 1 st each side this row,
then every 6 rows 6 times—54 sts.
Work even for 4 rows; pm each end of this row.
Continuing in St st, work 18 rows.*
Next Row: P9 and place on holder for Back
Bib; BO 29 sts; p16 and place on holder for
Front Bib.

Left Leg

Work from * to * of right Leg.
Next Row: P16 sts and place on holder for
Front Bib; BO 29 sts; p9 and place on
holder for Back Bib.

Pocket Lining

Using D, CO 22 sts; begin St st. (RS) Work even
for 17 rows; place sts on holder.

Front Bib

With RS facing, join yarn at Front Bib sts of left Leg; k16 Front Bib sts from left Leg holder, then knit across 16 Front Bib sts from right Leg holder—32 sts.

Knit even for 4 rows.

Next Row: (WS) Decrease 1 st each side— 30 sts remain.

Row 1: Knit.

Row 2: K3, p24, k3.

Rows 3–18: Repeat Rows 1 and 2.

Row 19: K4, BO 22 sts, k4.

Row 20: K3, p1, purl across 22 sts of Pocket Lining, p1, k3—30 sts.

Rows 21 and 22: Repeat Rows 1 and 2.

Rows 23–28: Knit.

BO all sts.

Back Bib

With RS facing, join yarn at Back bib sts of right Leg; k9 Back Bib sts from right Leg holder, then knit across 9 Back Bib sts of left Leg holder— 18 sts.

Rows 1, 3, and 5: K3, purl across to last 3 sts, k3.

Rows 2 and 4: Knit.

Row 6: K3, skp, purl to last 5 sts, k2tog, k3—16 sts remain.

Rows 7–23: Repeat Rows 1–6 twice, then Rows 1–5 once more—12 sts remain.

Row 24: K3, place sts on holder; BO 6 center sts; k3.

Straps

Continuing on last 3 sts, begin I-cord (see Special Techniques, page 175), making a strap that, when slightly stretched, fits over shoulder to attach to Front Bib.

K3tog, fasten off.

Join yarn to remaining 3 sts on holder; work as first Strap.

Finishing

Join Leg seams from lower edge to markers; join center Front and Back seams.

Sew Pocket Lining to WS of Bib; using back-stitch, make a divide in pocket (see photo).

Sew straps to Front Bib.

Side Panels (make 2)

With RS facing, pick up and knit 20 sts evenly between Front and Back Bibs; begin St st.

Work even for 14 rows; BO all sts.

Sew side seams, joining to sides of Front and Back bibs.

Repeat for other side.

Weave in ends.

Snowflake Bandana

Using F, CO 2 sts; begin Garter st.

Knit 1 row.

Shape Bandana: Increase 1 st each side this row, then every other row 28 times—60 sts.

Knit 1 row even.

Ties: CO 10 sts; knit 10 CO sts, k60, CO 10 sts —80 sts.

Knit 1 row; BO all sts. Weave in ends.

Embroider snowflake motif with contrasting scrap yarn (see photo).

Menorah Pillow

Hanukkah is the Jewish Festival of Lights, and its most recognizable symbol is the menorah—the nine-branched candelabra on which candles are lit and blessed, one by one, over the eight days of celebration. Contemporary menorahs are made from all kinds of materials—the elegant one on the front of this pillow is crafted from knitted cables in a luxurious blend of wool and cashmere, inviting rest for a holiday-weary head. The back of the pillow is worked in two pieces in double-moss stitch, then closed with knotted I-cord buttons. The menorah motif here was inspired by a candlestick design in *Charted Knitting Designs* by Barbara G. Walker.

FINISHED MEASUREMENTS
To fit 14" square pillow form snugly

MATERIALS
Debbie Bliss Cashmerino Aran (55% merino wool / 33% microfiber / 12% cashmere; 100 yards / 50 grams): 5 balls #300102 eggshell

NEEDLES
One pair straight needles size US 7 (4.5 mm)
Two 24" (60 cm) circular (circ) needles size US 6 (4 mm)
One set of double-pointed needles (dpn) size US 7 (4.5 mm)
Change needle size if necessary to obtain correct gauge.

NOTIONS
14" square pillow form, cable needle (cn), crochet hook size G/6 (4 mm), stitch holder, waste yarn, sewing needle, matching colored thread, yarn needle

GAUGE
21 sts and 32 rows = 4" (10 cm) using larger needles in Double-moss st after blocking

NOTES
✴ **Double-Moss Stitch**
(Multiple of 4 sts; 4-row repeat)
Rows 1 and 2: * P2, k2; repeat from * across.
Rows 3 and 4: * K2, p2; repeat from * across.
Repeat Rows 1–4 for Double-moss st.

Pillow

Front
Using larger needles and Provisional Chain CO (see Special Techniques, page 176), CO 76 sts; begin Double-moss st for lower border as follows:
Row 1 (RS): K3, * p2, k2; repeat from * to last 3 sts, end k3.
Row 2: P3, * k2, p2; repeat from * to last 3 sts, end p3.
Row 3: P3, * k2, p2; repeat from * to last 3 sts, end p3.
Row 4: K3, * p2, k2; repeat from * to last 3 sts, end k3.
Repeat Rows 1–4 once more.
Set-up Rows (RS): K3, p2, k2, p13, M1, k18, M1, k18, M1, p13, k2, p2, k3—79 sts.
Next Row: P3, k2, p2, place marker (pm); k14, p37, k14, pm; p2, k2, p3.
Maintaining 7 st border in Double-moss st on each side, begin Chart on center 65 sts. Work 97 rows of Chart. *Note: There is one decrease on the last row of the Chart*—76 sts remain.
Top Border: Work even for 8 rows in Double-moss st as for lower border. DO NOT BO. Break off yarn; leave sts on a spare thread.

menorah pillow

KEY

- Knit on RS, purl on WS
- Purl on RS, knit on WS
- No stitch
- Make 1 (knitwise)
- Make 1 (purlwise)
- Slip next st to cn, hold to back, k2, p1 from cn.
- Slip next 2 sts to cn, hold to front, p1, k2 from cn.
- Slip 2 sts to cn, hold to back, k2, k2 from cn.
- Slip 2 sts to cn, hold to front, k2, k2 from cn.
- Slip 2 sts to cn, hold to back, k2, p2 from cn.
- Slip 2 sts to cn, hold to front, p2, k2 from cn.
- Slip next st to cn, hold to back, k3, p1 from cn.
- Slip 3 sts to cn, hold to front, p1, k3 from cn.
- Slip 3 sts to cn, hold to back, k2, k3 from cn.
- Slip 2 sts to cn, hold to back, k3, p2 from cn.
- Slip 3 sts to cn, hold to front, p2, k3 from cn.
- Dcd (double centered dec) Slip 2 sts as if to k2tog to RH needle, k1, pass 2 slipped sts over knit st.
- P1, yo, p1 in next st to inc to 3 sts.
- 1 K1, [yo, k1] twice.
- 2 P5
- 3 K2, yo, k1, yo, k2
- 4 P7
- 5 K2, dcd, k2
- 6 K1, slip 1, k2tog, psso, k1
- 7 P3
- Ssk

Back

Lower Piece: Using larger needles and Provisional Chain CO (see Special Techniques, page 176), CO 76 sts; begin Double-moss st as for lower Front border.
Work even as established for 64 rows; BO all sts.

Upper Piece: Using larger needles and Provisional Chain CO, CO 76 sts; begin Double-moss st as for lower Back.
Work even for 8 rows.
(RS) Buttonhole Row: Continuing in pattern established, work 11 sts; [BO 3 sts, work 14 sts] 3 times, BO 3 sts; work to end (11 sts).
Next Row: Work 11 sts; CO 3 sts over BO sts of previous row by working 3 firm Backward Loop CO's (see Special Techniques, page 174); work to end. Work even as established for 64 rows. Do not BO. Break off yarn; leave sts on spare thread.

Finishing

Block Front piece to measure $14\frac{1}{2}$" square, and each Back piece to measure $14\frac{1}{2}$" x $8\frac{1}{4}$" by pinning to measurements with rustproof pins and misting well with cool water. Allow to air-dry. Place Upper Back piece over Lower Back piece, overlapping 16 rows at center; baste overlapped side edges together with sewing needle and thread.

Lower Seam

Carefully remove Provisional Chain CO from lower edge of Front by unpicking the first couple of sts of the crocheted chain, then unzipping the remainder. Place these sts on smaller circ needle. Do likewise for the Lower Back piece, placing the sts on second smaller circ needle.
With WS of pillow pieces together and Front facing, using a dpn and working yarn, CO 3 sts onto one of the circ needles.
Work 3-needle I-cord BO as follows:
* K2, slip 1, k2tog (one st each from Front and Back needles), psso to BO 1 st; return sts to left-hand needle. Repeat from * across, until one st remains on each circ needle; work corner as follows:
Work one row of unattached I-cord.
Work 3-needle I-cord BO for last pair of sts.
Work one row of unattached I-cord.
Place 3 sts on a holder while preparing sts for side seam.

Side Seam

With RS facing, working one st in from edge using smaller circ needle and a new length of working yarn, pick up and knit one st for each row along the right-hand side of Front. Break off new strand of yarn.
With RS facing, using second smaller circ needle and a new length of working yarn, pick up and knit one st for each row (the same number of sts as picked up along Front) along the left-hand side of Back, being sure to work through both layers where pieces overlap. Break off yarn.
With WS of Pillow pieces together, continue working 3-needle I-cord BO (for side seam) until one st remains on each circ needle; work corner as before.

Upper Seam

Remove sts from spare thread and place sts from top edge of Front on one circ needle and sts from Back on second circ needle. Continue to work 3-needle I-cord BO, until one st remains on each circ needle; work corner as before.

Side Seam

Work second side seam as for first; work corner as before. Break off yarn, leaving several inches. Do not BO. With yarn needle threaded with remaining yarn, neatly weave end of I-cord to beginning of I-cord. Remove basting thread from Back.

I-Cord Knot Buttons (Make 4)
Using dpn, CO 4 sts. Work I-cord for 6" (see Special Techniques, page 175). Tie into a large knot twice and tack ends onto WS of button. Sew buttons in place on lower piece of Back opposite buttonholes. Weave in all ends.

MICHELE ROSE ORNE *Floral Tree Skirt and Striped Stocking*

The inspiration for these coordinating pieces came from the beautiful handspun, kettle-dyed Uruguayan yarn used to knit them. The subtle variations of color, the bright floral motifs, and the pewter-button closure meld to form a multicultural look—part Turkish kilim rug, part Victorian tapestry, and part Icelandic cardigan. Leftover yarn from the skirt creates a fun-to-knit striped stocking, generously sized to hold plenty of goodies.

FINISHED MEASUREMENTS

Tree Skirt: approximately 60" diameter
Stocking: 7" wide opening; 16¾" from top to back of heel; 11½" from back of heel to tip of toe

YARN

Manos del Uruguay (100% handspun kettle-dyed wool; 135 yards / 100 grams): 5 skeins #66 red, 4 skeins #65 gold, 3 skeins #108 charcoal, 1 skein each #69 coral, #37 brown, #52 cream, #55 dark green, #67 chartreuse, #33 seafoam, #50 lilac, #115 ruby, #32 orchid, #67 medium green

NEEDLES

One pair straight needles size US 8 (5 mm)
One set of double-pointed needles (dpn) size US 8 (5 mm)
Change needle size if necessary to obtain correct gauge.

NOTIONS

Stitch markers, eight approximately ¾" buttons, yarn needle
Optional: Crochet hook size H/8 (5 mm) for Stocking hanger

GAUGE

Tree Skirt: 16 sts and 21 rows = 4" (10 cm) in Colorwork pattern from Chart
Stocking: 15 sts and 20 rows = 4" (10 cm) in Stockinette stitch (St st)

NOTES

✤ The Tree Skirt is knit in 4 separate panels. Each panel consists of 3 pie-shaped segments. Although the Chart appears to be three separate Charts, it is knit as one. Skip the spaces between each segment and continue to the next st in the adjacent segment.

✤ Carry colors loosely across back of work for border (stranded method; see Special Techniques, page 177); use separate balls of yarn for each color (intarsia method; see Special Techniques, page 175) for the floral section.

✤ Slip markers as you come to them.

Tree Skirt

3-Segment Panel (make 4)
Using red, CO 28 sts (counts as Row 1).
Rows 2 and 4: Knit.
Row 3 (RS): K9 (Segment 1), pm, k9 (Segment 2), pm, k10 (Segment 3).
Row 5—Increase Row: * K1, M1, work to marker following Chart; repeat from * twice—31 sts.
Continue following Chart, working increases into pattern every second and fourth rows as indicated on Chart—48 sts each in Segments 1 and 2, 49 sts in Segment 3; 145 total.
When Chart is complete, BO all sts using red.

Lace Border
Using red, CO 10 sts; begin Lace Border Chart. Work Rows 1–10 of Chart 76 times, or until piece is long enough to go around the entire outer circumference of the skirt. Lightly steam-block.

Finishing
Weave in loose ends on WS of each panel. Lightly steam-block each panel.

Assemble Tree Skirt: Lay 4 panels out into a circle; patterns should match up at the edges. With RS facing, sew 2 panels together, making sure to match up patterns at seams. Sew third panel to this piece; then sew fourth panel in same manner, leaving the 2 sides of the Tree Skirt open. On the open straight edges, work bands as follows:

Button Band: With RS facing, beginning at inner edge of Skirt using red, pick up and knit 86 sts along straight edge. Work even for 5 rows in Seed st. BO all sts loosely in pattern.

Buttonhole Band: On opposite straight edge, with RS facing, beginning at outer edge of Skirt using red, pick up and knit 86 sts. Work even for 2 rows in Seed st.

Buttonhole Row (WS): Work 3 sts in Seed st; [BO 2 sts, work 9 sts in Seed st] 7 times, BO 2 sts, work 4 sts in Seed st. Next Row (RS): Continuing in Seed st, CO 2 sts over BO sts of previous row.

Work 1 more row in Seed st; BO all sts.

Attach Lace Border: With RS facing, sew border onto the outer edge of the Skirt. Lightly steam-block border and panel seams. Sew buttons opposite buttonholes.

THE ORIGIN OF CHRISTMAS STOCKINGS

Long before he became immortalized as Saint Nick—so the legend goes—the kindly fourth-century bishop Nicholas of Myra made a practice of slipping into the houses of his poor parishioners and leaving gifts in their shoes. In one especially famous instance, Nicholas's heart went out to three sisters who wished to marry, but whose family was too poor to provide dowries. When the first two sisters were married, he secretly left a bag of gold in their shoes. But when the third sister was ready to marry, concerned that the family was on the lookout for him, he climbed onto the roof and dropped a bag of gold down the chimney. The bag landed in a stocking hung by the fireplace to dry—and ever since, in many cultures, stockings have been hung by fireplaces to be magically filled with gifts on Christmas Eve.

Still, there are some European and Latin American countries where shoes rather than stockings are laid out by the fire to receive treats. Sometimes, these shoes are filled with hay for Santa's reindeer or greens for the Three Kings' camels. In Scandinavia, families often make a point of placing all their shoes side by side on Christmas Eve, in hope of ensuring family harmony for the coming year.

Stocking

Leg

Using red, CO 54 sts. Working back and forth, begin Leg Chart. When Chart is complete, break off coral and begin Heel.

Heel Flap

Note: Heel is worked on first and last 13 sts.
With WS of Leg facing, slip first 13 sts to dpn, place center 28 sts on holder for Instep, join red and work in St st across remaining 13 sts. Slip sts on dpn to right-hand end of needle and work across sts from dpn (what was the first st on dpn is now the thirteenth st on the right-hand needle)—26 sts on the right-hand needle. Working on Heel sts only; work even until Heel flap measures $2\frac{1}{2}$" from beginning, ending after a RS row.

Turn Heel

Row 1: P15, p2tog, p1, turn.
Row 2: Slip 1, k5, k2tog, k1, turn.
Row 3: Slip 1, purl to 1 st before gap, p2tog (the sts on either side of gap), p1, turn.
Row 4: Slip 1, knit to 1 st before gap, skp (the sts on either side of gap), k1, turn.
Repeat Rows 3 and 4 until all sts have been worked—16 sts remain.
Work 1 WS row even.

Heel Gusset

Change to dpns; join dark green. Continuing in St st, work across first 8 sts of Heel, transfer these sts onto spare needle; with Needle 1, work across next 8 sts, on same needle, pick up and knit 10 sts along left side of Heel Flap—18 sts on Needle 1; transfer 28 sts from st holder to Needles 2 and 3—14 sts each needle; with Needle 4, pick up and knit 10 sts along right side of Heel Flap, work across 8 sts from spare needle—18 sts on Needle 4; pm for beginning of rnd.
Note: From this point on, follow the color sequence on Foot Chart. In order to minimize the disruption of the color patterns at the beginning and end of each round, work a Jogless Color Change (see Special Techniques, page 175).
Knit 1 rnd.
Shape Gusset: Beginning with Rnd 3 of Foot Chart, work decreases as follows:
Rnd 1: On Needle 1, work across to last 3 sts, k2tog, k1; work across Needles 2 and 3; on Needle 4, k1, ssk, work to end.
Rnd 2: Continuing to follow Chart for color sequence, work one rnd even.
Repeat Rnds 1 and 2 until there are 13 sts each on Needles 1 and 4 and 14 sts each on Needles 2 and 3—54 sts total.

Foot

Work even until Row 33 of Foot Chart is complete.

Shape Toe

Rnd 1—Decrease Rnd: * On Needle 1, work to last 3 sts, k2tog, k1; on Needle 2, k1, ssk, work across; repeat from * on Needles 3 and 4.
Rnd 2: Continuing to follow Foot Chart for color sequence, work one rnd even.
Repeat Rnds 1 and 2 until 18 sts remain after a Decrease rnd.
With Needle 4, work sts on Needle 1; slip sts on Needle 2 onto Needle 3; graft sts together using Kitchener st (see Special Techniques, page 176).

Finishing

Weave in all loose ends. With color of choice, sew open seam closed. Using red, chartreuse, and cream, crochet or braid a loop and attach at back of Leg for hanging the Stocking. Lightly steam-block the completed Stocking.

tree skirt
COLORWORK CHART

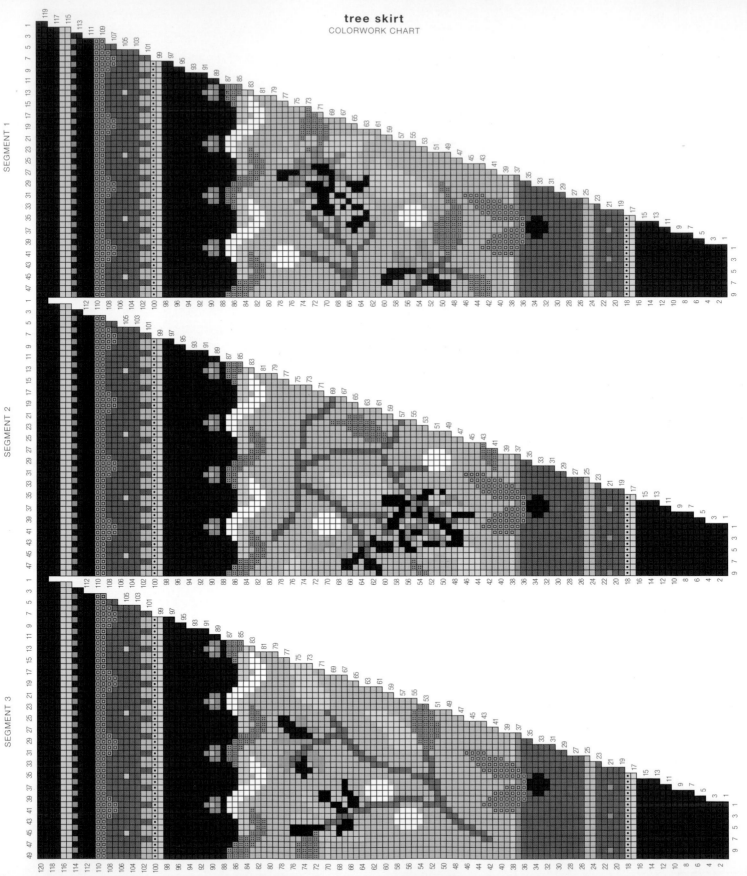

stocking
LEG CHART

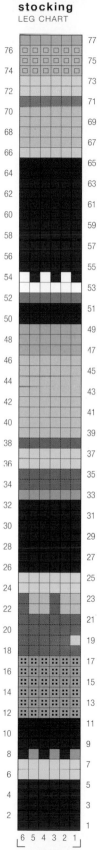

6-st repeat

stocking
FOOT CHART

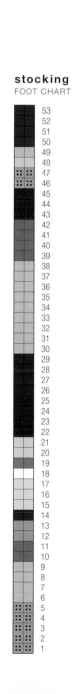

tree skirt
LACE BORDER CHART

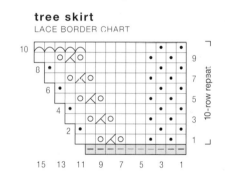

10-row repeat

TREE SKIRT AND STOCKING COLOR KEY

Knit on RS, purl on WS except as indicated.

- ■ red
- ■ red—knit on WS
- ☐ chartreuse
- ☐ chartreuse—knit on WS
- ☐ lilac
- ☐ gold
- ☐ orchid
- ☐ brown
- ☐ cream
- ■ ruby
- ■ ruby—knit on WS
- ☐ seafoam
- ☐ medium green
- ☐ dark green
- ☐ charcoal
- ☐ coral

TREE SKIRT KEY

- ☐ Knit on RS, purl on WS
- ☐ Purl on RS, knit on WS
- ☐ Yo
- ☐ K2tog
- ☐ Bind off 1 stitch
- ☐ Cast-on row

TEVA DURHAM

Aran Tree Skirt and Stocking

What better way is there for a knitter to honor her solstice evergreen than to dress it up in a thick, cabled skirt and hang a matching stocking nearby? A bulky Icelandic wool yarn is doubled to give these pieces an ultra-handcrafted look and to speed up the knitting.

FINISHED MEASUREMENTS

Tree Skirt: 55" diameter
Stocking: 10" wide opening; 22" long

YARN

Reynolds Lopi (100% Icelandic wool; 117 yards / 3.5 ounces): #718 off-white (MC) and #367 mauve-gray (CC) (use double strand throughout)
Tree skirt: 17 balls MC; 4 balls CC
Stocking: 3 balls MC; 1 ball CC

NEEDLES

One 24" circular (circ) needle size US 13 (9 mm)
One 16" circular needle size US 13 (9 mm)
Change needle size if necessary to obtain correct gauge.

NOTIONS

Two cable needles (cn), yarn needle, stitch marker, crochet hook size K/10.5 (6.5 mm)

GAUGE

10 sts and 16 rows = 4" (10 cm) in Stockinette stitch (St st) using 2 strands held together

NOTES

⊕ Tree Skirt is worked from radius of circle around, using Short Rows to shape wedge-like segments. On each Row 1 of Chart (after the first repeat), knit the wraps together with the wrapped sts (see Special Techniques, page 177) for all knit sts; the wraps on the purl sts may be worked with the wrapped sts if desired, but it is not necessary as these wraps blend in.

⊕ The Tree Skirt Cable Chart shows one segment; the Cable repeats are designed to meet between segments.

⊕ The contrast color (CC) trim is worked at the same time, using Intarsia method (See Special Techniques, page 175). It is then extended along CO and BO edges to form a tie to go around the tree trunk.

Tree Skirt

Segment 1: Using 24" circ needle and 2 strands MC held together, CO 67 sts; using 2 strands CC held together, CO 6 sts—73 sts total. (RS) Working back and forth, begin Cable Tree Skirt Chart Row 1, working Sts 1–6 with CC and Sts 7–73 with MC, twisting yarn between colors to prevent holes.
Short Row Shaping: On Row 5 of Chart, begin Short Rows as follows:
(RS) Work across to last st shown on Chart, wrap next stitch, turn (wrp-t).
(WS) Leaving 3 sts unworked at end of row, work to end as indicated on Chart.
Continue in this manner through Row 50 of Chart.
Segment 2: Working wraps together with wrapped sts as explained in Notes at left, begin Row 1 of Chart across all sts. Work Rows 1–50 as for Segment 1.
Segments 3–10: Work as for Segment 2.
Segment 11 (final segment): Work as for Segment 2 through Row 40, to make the angle of the edge less severe (to better match the CO row); BO while working Row 1 of Chart, working wraps together with wrapped sts.

Finishing

Ties: Using 2 strands CC, pick up and knit 6 sts at end or beginning of CC Cable. Continue in pattern as established until tie is length of open edge, plus 16" more, ending with 4 rows in St st. BO all sts. Sew cable trim along open edge, leaving remaining 16" free. Repeat on other side. Weave in ends. Block lightly.

Stocking

Using 16" circ needle and 2 strands MC held together, CO 48 sts. Join for working in the rnd, being careful not to twist sts; place marker (pm) for beginning of rnd.

Work Rnds 1–39 of Leg Chart, shaping as indicated on Chart—36 sts remain.

Rnd 40: Divide for Heel—work around to 5 sts before the end of the rnd; slip last 20 sts worked onto st holder for Instep (see Chart). Heel will be worked on remaining 16 sts.

Heel

Row 1 (RS): * P2tog, [k1, p1] twice, k1; repeat from * once, p2tog, turn—13 sts remain.

Row 2: Work in k1, p1 rib—knit the knits and purl the purls as they face you.

Repeat Row 2 until Heel measures 2½" from Dividing Row, ending with a WS row.

Turn Heel

(RS) Change to St st, work 8 sts, wrp-t; work 3 sts, wrp-t; * work to one st past previous wrap, wrp-t; repeat from * until 3 wraps have been worked at each side, working to end of WS row.

Instep and Foot

(RS) K13 heel sts; pick up and knit 6 sts along side edge of Heel Flap; work across 20 sts of Instep, following Rnd 41 of Chart; pick up and knit 6 sts along opposite side edge of Heel Flap—45 sts.

Continue even as established, working St st on Sole, Cables and Rev St st on Instep, with 2 St sts on either side of Instep, until foot measures 7" from Heel or desired length, and AT THE SAME TIME,

Shape Foot: Decrease Rnd—Knit to 1 st before Instep sts; k2tog, work 20 Instep sts, ssk; knit to end of rnd. Repeat Decrease Rnd every other rnd 6 times total—30 sts remain (13 for the Sole, 17 for the Instep, after working all decreases from Chart).

Toe

K11, k2tog, pm, ssk, p13, k2tog, pm, ssk— 28 sts remain.

Decrease Rnd: * Work to 2 sts before marker, k2tog, ssk; repeat from * around. Repeat Decrease Rnd until 12 sts remain. Graft Toe sts together with Kitchener st (see Special Techniques, page 176).

Finishing

Cable Trim: Using 2 strands CC, CO 6 sts. Work Cable as for Sts 1–6 of Leg Chart until piece measures same as CO edge, ending with 4 rows St st. BO all sts.

Beginning at center back of Stocking, sew Cable trim around edge, then graft CO and BO sts together. Weave in ends. Block lightly. Using crochet hook and single strand CC, work a 5" crochet chain (see Special Techniques, page 174); fasten off, leaving a tail for attaching chain to Stocking. Sew chain to inside center back of trim.

tree skirt
CABLE CHART

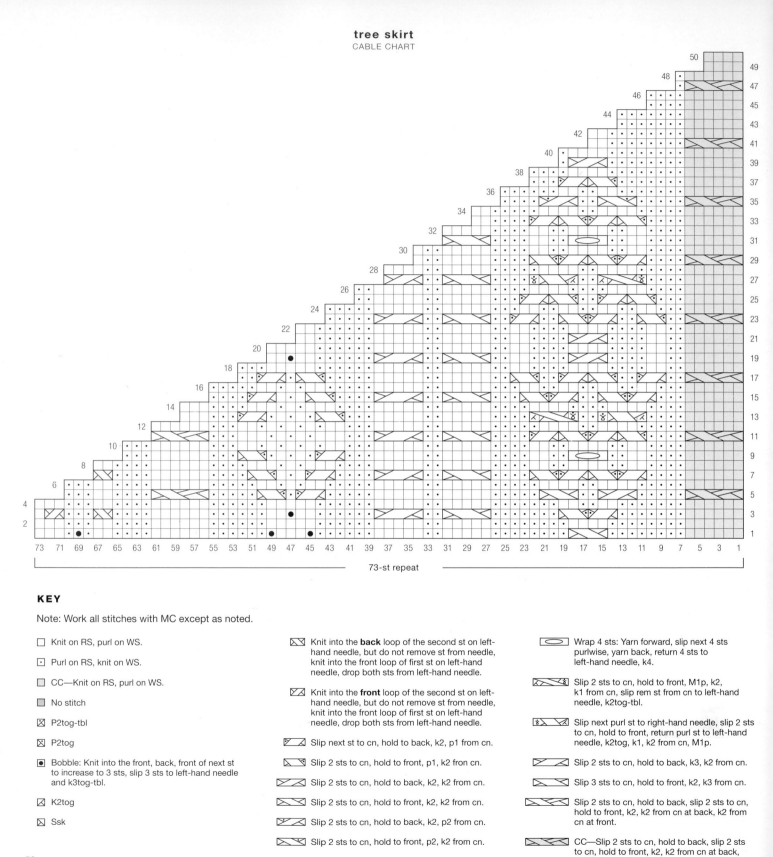

73-st repeat

KEY

Note: Work all stitches with MC except as noted.

☐ Knit on RS, purl on WS.

⊡ Purl on RS, knit on WS.

▦ CC—Knit on RS, purl on WS.

▨ No stitch

⊠ P2tog-tbl

⊠ P2tog

● Bobble: Knit into the front, back, front of next st to increase to 3 sts, slip 3 sts to left-hand needle and k3tog-tbl.

⊠ K2tog

⊠ Ssk

⊠ Knit into the **back** loop of the second st on left-hand needle, but do not remove st from needle, knit into the front loop of first st on left-hand needle, drop both sts from left-hand needle.

⊠ Knit into the **front** loop of the second st on left-hand needle, but do not remove st from needle, knit into the front loop of first st on left-hand needle, drop both sts from left-hand needle.

▱ Slip next st to cn, hold to back, k2, p1 from cn.

▱ Slip 2 sts to cn, hold to front, p1, k2 fron cn.

▱ Slip 2 sts to cn, hold to back, k2, k2 from cn.

▱ Slip 2 sts to cn, hold to front, k2, k2 from cn.

▱ Slip 2 sts to cn, hold to back, k2, p2 from cn.

▱ Slip 2 sts to cn, hold to front, p2, k2 from cn.

⬯ Wrap 4 sts: Yarn forward, slip next 4 sts purlwise, yarn back, return 4 sts to left-hand needle, k4.

▱ Slip 2 sts to cn, hold to front, M1p, k2, k1 from cn, slip rem st from cn to left-hand needle, k2tog-tbl.

▱ Slip next purl st to right-hand needle, slip 2 sts to cn, hold to front, return purl st to left-hand needle, k2tog, k1, k2 from cn, M1p.

▱ Slip 2 sts to cn, hold to back, k3, k2 from cn.

▱ Slip 3 sts to cn, hold to front, k2, k3 from cn.

▱ Slip 2 sts to cn, hold to back, slip 2 sts to cn, hold to front, k2, k2 from cn at back, k2 from cn at front.

▱ CC—Slip 2 sts to cn, hold to back, slip 2 sts to cn, hold to front, k2, k2 from cn at back, k2 from cn at front.

stocking
INSTEP CHART

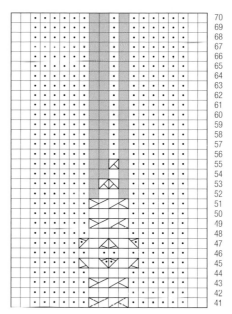

stocking
LEG CHART

Heel stitches   Heel stitches

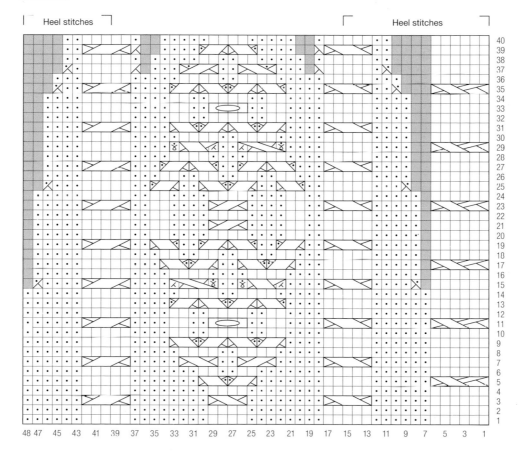

CINDY TAYLOR *Mrs. Claus Doll*

Santa may get all the credit on Christmas Eve, but we know that behind nearly every great man, there's a woman who's really running the show. It's time to give Mrs. Claus her due. After generations of keeping the elves in line, collating the Christmas lists, and baking enough cookies to feed an army, she's honored here by Cindy Taylor in a very soft, very cuddly doll, complete with knitted-on high-heeled boots and a choice of petticoats and dresses. Mrs. Claus does not scrimp on style.

FINISHED MEASUREMENT
Approximately 16" tall

YARN
Mission Falls 1824 Wool (100% wool; 85 yards / 50 grams): 1 skein each in black (A), pink (D), blue (E), wine (F), olive (G), and gold (H)
Mission Falls 1824 Cotton (100% cotton; 84 yards / 50 grams): 1 skein each in ivory (B) and flax (C)
Shown in the following colors:
Boots (A); Body (B); hair (C); solid dress (D); 2-color dress (G and H); petticoat (D, E, and F)

NEEDLES
One set of five double-pointed needles (dpn) size US 7 (4.5 mm)
Change needle size if necessary to obtain correct gauge.

NOTIONS
Yarn needle, polyester fiberfill, crochet hook size H/8 (5 mm), 2 buttons for dress, scrap embroidery floss for eyes and mouth, embroidery needle, 1¼" plastic ring for hair bun

GAUGE
16 sts and 24 rows = 4" (10 cm) in Stockinette stitch (St st)

Doll

Boots (make 2)
Boot Heel
Using 2 dpn and A, CO 9 sts; begin St st. (WS) Beginning with a purl row, work even for 5 rows; cut yarn, leaving heel sts on needle.
First Side: Continuing with A, on same needle, CO 6 sts. Working on these 6 sts only:
Row 1 (WS): Purl across to last st, M1, p1.
Row 2: K1, M1, knit to end.
Repeat Rows 1 and 2 once—10 sts.
(WS) Purl side sts, then heel sts—19 sts total.
Second Side: Using A, on a separate needle, CO 6 sts. Working on these 6 sts only:
Row 1 (WS): P1, M1, purl to end.
Row 2: Knit across to last st, M1, k1.
Repeat Rows 1 and 2 once—10 sts.
(WS) Continuing with first needle, purl sts of second side—29 sts.
Toe Shaping: Continue on all Boot sts;
Row 1 (RS): K1, ssk, knit across to last 3 sts, k2tog, k1.
Row 2: P1, p2tog, purl across to last 3 sts, p2tog-tbl, p1.
Repeat Rows 1 and 2 once—21 sts.
Boot Top
Divide sts evenly onto 3 needles. Join for working in the rnd; place marker (pm) for beginning of rnd. Work 3 rnds even; break off A.

Legs (make 2)
Join B; continuing in St st, work even for 6". BO all sts; sew boot and leg seams; stuff.

Body
Using B, CO 36 sts; divide evenly onto 3 needles. Join for working in the rnd, being careful not to twist sts; pm for beginning of rnd. Begin St st. Work even until piece measures 4½" from beginning.
Shape Shoulders: Divide sts evenly onto 2 needles; turn Body WS out. Using 3-Needle BO method (see Special Techniques, page 177), BO 5 sts at beginning of next 2 rows— 16 sts remain for neck; 8 on each needle. Turn Body RS out.

Neck
Dividing sts evenly onto 3 needles on first rnd, knit even for 4 rnds.

Head

Divide sts evenly onto 2 needles.

Rnd 1: On first needle— * K1, M1, knit across to last st, M1, k1; repeat from * on second needle—20 sts.

Rnd 2: Knit.

Rnds 3–8: Repeat Rnds 1 and 2—32 sts.

Rnds 9–12: Knit.

Rnd 13: On first needle— * K1, ssk, knit to last 3 sts on needle, k2tog, k1; repeat from * on second needle—28 sts remain.

Rnd 14: Knit.

Rnds 15–20: Repeat Rnds 13 and 14— 16 sts remain.

Graft remaining sts together using Kitchener st (see Special Techniques, page 176); stuff piece loosely.

Arms (make 2)

Using B, CO 18 sts; divide sts evenly onto 3 needles. Join for working in the rnd, being careful not to twist sts; pm for beginning of rnd. Begin St st.

Work even until piece measures 4" from the beginning.

Shape Hands: Divide sts evenly onto 2 needles.

Rnd 1: On first needle— * K1, M1, knit across to last st, M1, k1; repeat from * on second needle—22 sts.

Rnd 2: Knit.

Repeat Rnds 1 and 2 once—26 sts.

Knit even for 4 rnds.

Hand

Rnd 1: On first needle— * K1, ssk, knit across to last 3 sts, k2tog, k1; repeat from * on second needle—22 sts remain.

Rnd 2: Knit.

Repeat Rnds 1 and 2 three times—10 sts remain. Graft sts together using Kitchener st and stuff piece loosely.

Thumb

Using B, pick up and knit 6 sts at upper base of Hand; divide evenly onto 3 needles. Join for working in the rnd; pm for beginning of rnd. Begin St st. Work even for 3 rnds.

Next Rnd: * [K2tog] 3 times *; stuff Thumb.

Knit 1 rnd even.

Next Rnd: K1, k2tog.

Break off yarn. Thread through remaining sts; pull to close; fasten off.

Finishing

Sew arms and legs to body, being careful to position hands and feet correctly.

To make hair, using C, beginning and ending at end of Head increases (see photo), stitch through and wrap outer perimeter of head.

To make bun, using plastic ring, crochet hook, and C, work single crochet (sc) around the ring. Using yarn needle threaded with C, wrap ring with yarn, going in and out of center, until bun is approximately 2" in diameter; attach Bun by sewing to back of hairline.

Using embroidery floss, sew eyes and mouth as desired (see photo).

Clothes

Petticoat

Using color of choice, CO 48 sts; divide evenly over 3 needles. Join for working in the rnd; pm for beginning of rnd. Begin St st.
Work even until piece measures 4" from the beginning, ending 2 sts before marker on last row.
Shape Armholes: Divide sts evenly onto 2 needles. * BO off 4 sts (1 st remaining on needle); using same needle, k19—20 sts on needle. Repeat from * with second needle; turn.
Front and Back Yoke (both alike)
Working on second needle sts only,
Row 1 (WS): * Purl.
Row 2: K1, ssk, knit to last 3 sts, k2tog, k1.
Repeat Rows 1 and 2 twice—14 sts remain.
Rows 7–9: Work even in St st.
BO all sts, leaving a 10" tail.
Repeat from * for sts on first needle.
Join Shoulders: Using crochet hook and 10" tail, chain (ch) 10; join with slip st to opposite side.

Crochet Trim

Armhole: * Join color of choice at center of the underarm (4 BO sts). Sc in next 2 sts, half double crochet (hdc) up side of armhole to shoulder chain; sc in each chain; hdc down side of armhole, sc in last 2 sts. Fasten off. Repeat from * for remaining armhole.
Edging: Join color of choice in "side seam" st on lower edge.
Rnd 1: Ch 1, sc in each st around; join with slip st to first st—48 sc.
Rnd 2: Ch 3 (counts as double crochet [dc]), dc each sc around; join with slip st to top of ch-3.
Rnd 3: [Ch 3, slip st in next st] around; join with slip st to ch-3.

Dress

Skirt

Using color of choice, (D [solid]; G [2-color] as shown), CO 90 sts; divide evenly onto 3 needles. Join for working in the rnd, being careful not to twist sts; pm for beginning of rnd.
Begin St st.
Work even for 4 rnds.
Eyelet Rnd: * Yo, k2tog; rep from * around.
Knit 1 rnd even.
Begin Cat's Paw Chart, Rnd 1. Working 9-st repeat 10 times around, work Rows 1–6 once.
Repeat Eyelet Rnd once.
Work even for 4 rnds.

Bodice

Using color of choice, (D [solid]; H [2-color] as shown), continue as follows:
Rnd 1: * K1, k2tog; repeat from * around— 60 sts remain, and AT THE SAME TIME,
Solid version: Work Rnd 1, then work 2 rnds even.
2-color version: Work Rnd 1 in color pattern as follows: K3 G, k1 H, * k5 G, k1 H; repeat from * to last 2 sts, end k2 G, then work Rnds 2 and 3.
Rnd 2: K2 G, * k3 H, k3 G; repeat from * to last 4 sts, k3 H, k1 H.
Rnd 3: K1 G * k5 H, k1 G; repeat from * to last 5 sts, k5 H.
Front Opening: (Both versions) Continuing in Bodice color as established,
Row 1 (RS): BO 2 sts, knit to end of row, turn.
Row 2: Purl.
Row 3: Knit.
Repeat Rows 2 and 3 until piece measures 4½"

CAT'S PAW CHART

L— 9-st repeat —J

KEY

☐	Knit
☉	Yo
⧅	K2tog

from CO edge, ending with a WS row.

Shape Armholes: K11 for right Front; BO 2 sts for armhole; k24 for Back; BO 2 sts for armhole (1 st remaining on needle); k10 for left Front.

Left Front

Working on left Front sts only:

Row 1 and all WS rows: Slip 1, purl to end.

Row 2: K1, ssk, k8—10 sts remain.

Row 4: K1, ssk, k7—9 sts remain.

Row 6: Knit across to last 3 sts, k2tog, k1.

Row 7: Repeat Row 1.

Repeat Rows 6 and 7 twice—6 sts remain.

Place remaining sts on holder.

Back

Working on Back sts only:

Row 1 (WS): Join yarn and purl to end.

Row 2: K1, ssk, knit across to last 3 sts, k2tog, k1—22 sts remain.

Row 3: Purl.

Rows 4 and 5: Repeat Rows 2 and 3—20 sts remain after Row 4.

Row 6: Knit.

Row 7: Purl.

Repeat Rows 6 and 7 twice. Place remaining sts on holder.

Right Front

Working on right Front sts only:

Row 1 (WS): Join yarn and purl to end.

Row 2: Slip 1, knit across to last 3 sts, k2tog, k1—10 sts remain.

Row 3: Purl.

Rows 4 and 5: Repeat Rows 2 and 3—9 sts remain after Row 4.

Row 6: Slip 1, ssk, knit to end—8 sts remain.

Row 7: Purl.

Repeat Rows 6 and 7 twice—6 sts remain.

Turn dress WS out; work 3-needle BO over 6 sts at each shoulder, keeping center 8 sts of Back on holder for neck. Turn dress RS out.

Sleeves

Using Bodice color, with RS facing, beginning at center of underarm, pick up and knit 25 sts evenly around armhole; divide evenly onto 3 needles. Join for working in the rnd; pm for beginning of rnd.

Puff Sleeves (solid color version)

Rnd 1: K9, k1-f/b of next 7 sts, k9—32 sts.

Rnds 2–4: Knit.

Rnd 5: * K1, ssk, knit to last 3 sts, k2tog, k1—30 sts remain.

Rnds 6–9: Knit.

Rnds 10–14: Repeat Rnds 5–9—28 sts remain after Rnd 10.

Rnds 15 and 16: Repeat Rnds 5 and 6—26 sts remain after Rnd 15.

Bind off remaining sts.

Straight Sleeves (2-color version)

Work even for 16 rnds; BO remaining sts.

Finishing

Crochet Trim for Sleeves

Rnd 1: Using Sleeve color, or color of choice and crochet hook, sc evenly around lower edge of Sleeve; join with Slip st to first st.

Rnd 2: * Ch 3, Slip st in next st; rep from * around; join with Slip st to first st. Fasten off.

Crochet Trim for Skirt

Rnd 1: Using Skirt color or color of choice and crochet hook, sc evenly around lower edge of skirt; join with Slip st to first st—90 sc.

Rnd 2: * Work Shell st [sc, hdc, dc, hdc, sc in same st] in next sc, ch 1, skip 2 sc; repeat from * around. Fasten off.

Crochet Trim for Neck Opening

Row 1: With RS facing, beginning at center of Right Front neck opening, sc evenly around neck, ending at center Left Front, including sts on holder for Back neck. Fasten off.

Buttonholes: To make 2 buttonholes, with RS facing, beginning at center of Right Front neck as Row 1, slip st in first sc, ch 3, skip 2 sc, slip st in next 6 sc, ch 3, skip 2 sc, slip st in next sc. Fasten off.

When weaving in ends, tack lower edge of Right Front band over Left Front band. Sew buttons opposite chain loop buttonholes.

Winter Solstice Table Runners

These sophisticated table runners are a beautiful way to "dress" the holiday table. The center gray one is embellished with sashiko—a Japanese form of running-stitch embroidery—in a harmonious design that can be interpreted in many ways. The intersecting circles can recall the arc of the sun's path, the cycles of the seasons, the encircling embrace of a loved one, or even poinsettias. The lace pattern of the two taupe side table runners resemble candle flames; the optional embroidered stars are inspired by huck embroidery.

FINISHED MEASUREMENTS
Sashiko version:
Approximately 16" wide by 55" long
Openwork version:
Approximately 16" wide by 48" long

YARNS
Louet Gems Merino Opal (100% merino wool; 112 yards / 50 grams):
Sashiko version:
7 skeins #43 taupe (MC)
Openwork version:
6 skeins #36 linen grey (MC)
Both versions:
Louet Euroflax Sportweight (100% linen; 135 yards / 50 grams): 2 skeins #18.36 natural (CC)

NEEDLES
One 40" circular (circ) needle size US 3 (3.25 mm)
One 40" circular needle size US 2 (2.75 mm)
Change needle size if necessary to obtain correct gauge.

NOTIONS
Both versions: Yarn needle
Sashiko version only: Tissue paper, 10" wide by 54" long, dressmaker's tracing wheel, sharp, large-eyed embroidery needle

GAUGE
24 sts and 36 rows = 4" (10 cm) in Openwork pattern, using larger needles and MC
25 sts and 34 rows = 4" (10 cm) in Stockinette stitch (St st), using larger needles and MC

NOTES
✳ **Openwork Stitch Pattern**
(Multiple of 12 sts + 3; 16-row repeat)
(See Chart)
Row 1 and all WS rows: Purl.
Row 2 (RS): K1 (edge st), * k1, yo, k2, k2tog, k3, ssk, k2, yo; repeat from * across, end k2 (edge sts).
Row 4: K1, * k2, yo, k2, k2tog, k1, ssk, k2, yo, k1; repeat from * across, end k2.
Row 6: K1, * k3, yo, k1, k2tog, k1, ssk, k1, yo, k2; repeat from * across, end k2.
Row 8: Knit.
Row 10: K1, * k2, ssk, k2, yo, k1, yo, k2, k2tog, k1; repeat from * across, end k2.
Row 12: K1, * k1, ssk, k2, yo, k3, yo, k2, k2tog; repeat from * across, end k2.
Row 14: K1, * k1, ssk, k1, yo, k5, yo, k1, k2tog; repeat from * across, end k2.
Row 16: Knit.
Repeat Rows 1–16 for Openwork pattern.

OPENWORK CHART

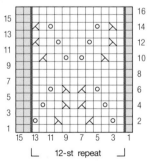

⌐ 12-st repeat ⌐

KEY
☐ MC-Knit on RS, purl on WS.
⊡ Yo
⊠ K2tog
⊠ Ssk
☐ Edge sts

WINTER SOLSTICE

On or around December 22, in the thick of the holiday season, comes the winter solstice—scientifically speaking, the point at which the earth is tilted so the northern hemisphere receives the least amount of sunlight. While it is the shortest day of the year in this half of the world, it is also the day that marks the return of the sun; every day after it will be longer. For many people, from ancient times to the present, this turning point has been a cause for celebration as it marks the subtle exchange of darkness for light, cold for warmth, despair for joy. In fact, many of our modern holiday traditions hark back to this natural event—lighting candles, Christmas tree lights, and fires; bringing greenery and special plants into our homes; and feasting in celebration of harvest abundance. Even gift-giving stems from the solstice event, a show of appreciation for the company of family and friends during a dark, cold season—a good thing to remember when battling the shopping crowds.

Sashiko Table Runner

Sashiko Table Runner

Using Long-Tail CO method (see Special Techniques, page 176) and MC, CO 91 sts; begin St st. Work even until piece measures 52" from the beginning, ending with a RS row. BO all sts using Outline Stitch BO (see Special Techniques, page 176).

Openwork Table Runner

Using Long-Tail CO method (see Special Techniques, page 176) and MC, CO 87 sts; begin Openwork pattern. Work Rows 1–16 of pattern 23 times—368 rows. BO all sts using Outline Stitch BO.

Openwork Table Runner

Finishing (both versions)

With yarn threaded on a tapestry needle, weave in loose ends. Wet-block to finished measurements.

Apply edging on both versions; numbers in ( ) apply to Sashiko version.

Edging: With RS facing, using larger needles and CC, pick up and knit 796 (932) sts as follows: 84 (88) sts in horizontal loops along CO row, place marker (pm); 314 (378) sts along side, pm; 84 (88) sts in horizontal loops along BO row, pm; 314 (378) sts along remaining side. Join for working in the rnd; pm to indicate beginning of rnd.

Note: Slip markers as you come to them.

Rnd 1: Purl.

Rnds 2 and 4: [K1-tbl, knit to one st before marker, k1-tbl] 4 times.

Rnd 3: [K1 tbl, yo, * k2tog, yo; repeat from * to one st before marker, k1-tbl] 4 times.

Rnd 5: [K1-tbl, yo, * k1, slip 1 wyif; repeat from * to 2 sts before marker, k1, yo, k1-tbl] 4 times.

Rnd 6: [K1-tbl, * k1, slip 1 wyif; repeat from * to 2 sts before marker, k1, k1-tbl] 4 times.

Rnd 7: [K1-tbl, yo, k2, * slip 1 wyif, k1; repeat from * to 2 sts before marker, k1, yo, k1-tbl] 4 times.

Rnds 8 and 12: [K1-tbl, k1, * k1, slip 1 wyif; repeat from * to 3 sts before marker, k2, k1-tbl] 4 times.

Rnd 9: [K1-tbl, yo, * k1, slip 1 wyif; repeat from * to 2 sts before marker, k1, yo, k1-tbl] 4 times.

Rnd 10: [K1-tbl, * k1, slip 1 wyif; repeat from * to 2 sts before marker, k1, k1-tbl] 4 times.

Rnd 11: [K1-tbl, yo, k1, * k1, slip 1 wyif; repeat from * to 3 sts before marker, k2, yo, k1-tbl] 4 times.

Change to smaller needles; purl even for 2 rnds.

Next Rnd: * P1, slip 1 wyib; repeat from * to end.

BO as follows: Slip 2 sts to right-hand needle and, with tip of left-hand needle, * pass the first st over the second stitch, slip 1; repeat from * across.

SASHIKO EMBROIDERY

Draw 3 lines on tissue paper: one in the center, lengthwise, and two on either side spaced 1¾" from center. On first and third lines, make marks 1" from bottom, and 13 more spaced 1¾" apart. On center line, make mark 2¾" from bottom, and 13 more spaced 1¾" apart. Using a compass set at 1¾", draw circles on all marks (top and bottom circles on outside lines will be halved). Trace lines using a dressmaker's tracing wheel. Baste paper pattern to RS of St st runner and, using CC and a sharp embroidery needle and holes left by wheel as guide, embroider design using a running stitch. Remove paper pattern carefully once embroidery is complete and weave in ends. Steam lightly.

OPENWORK EMBROIDERY

Thread a 12" length of CC yarn onto yarn needle. Beginning with a corner lozenge (see Embroidery Chart), locate the center st (pink on the Chart). Bring needle up left side of this stitch, leaving a 3–4" tail on WS; run through third st to the left (gold on the Chart) and through the st directly above the gold stitch (green on the Chart). Run through center st again. Repeat this step on right-hand side. Continue running linen yarn through marked sts (gold on the Chart), always running yarn through center st after each step. Bring yarn back to WS and knot ends together. Repeat on remainder of runner, leaving neighboring lozenges unworked (see photo). Steam lightly.

OPENWORK EMBROIDERY CHART

KEY

☐ CC: center st for Embroidery

☐ CC: see Embroidery instructions

☐ CC: see Embroidery instructions

JO SHARP *Regal Frost Cushions*

On a cold winter evening, after a holiday feast or a snowball fight, nothing feels better than snuggling down before a crackling fire. When you do, you'll want to surround yourself with these thick, tweedy, frost-patterned cushions in rich, regal colors dressed up with details like a twisted cord edging or silky tassels.

FINISHED MEASUREMENTS
Cushions 1 and 2: 20" square;
Cushion 3: 25" square

YARN
Jo Sharp Classic DK Wool (100% wool;
107 yards / 50 grams)
Jo Sharp Silkroad DK Tweed (85% merino wool /
10% silk / 5% cashmere; 147 yards / 50 grams)
Jo Sharp Silkroad Aran Tweed (85% merino
wool / 10% silk / 5% cashmere; 93 yards /
50 grams)
Cushion 1: Classic DK Wool: 7 balls #323
antique (ivory; A), 4 balls #322 ginger (B)
Cushion 2: Silkroad DK Tweed: 5 balls #405
emporio (A), Classic DK Wool Heather: 2 balls
#912 brocade (B)
Cushion 3: Silkroad Aran Tweed: 6 balls #116
ivy (A), 3 balls #114 vermouth (ivory; B)

NEEDLES
Cushions 1 and 2: One pair straight needles
size US 6 (4 mm)
Cushion 3: One pair straight needles size
US 8 (5 mm)

NOTIONS
Cushions 1 and 2: One 22" square
cushion insert
Cushion 2: Four 4" nylon tassels
Cushion 3: One 26" square cushion insert

GAUGE
Cushions 1 and 2: 22 sts and 30 rows = 4"
(10 cm) in stitch pattern from Chart using
smaller needles
Cushion 3: 18 sts and 24 rows = 4" (10 cm) in
stitch pattern from Chart using larger needles

*Cushion styles shown
(clockwise from top left):
1, 2, 3*

Cushion

Front
Using A and smaller (smaller, larger) needles,
CO 110 sts; begin St st and Chart.
(RS) Carrying color not in use loosely across
the WS of piece, work Rows 1–150 from Chart
(see page 62).
BO all sts loosely.

Back
Using A and smaller (smaller, larger) needles,
CO 110 sts; begin St st. Work even for 150
rows. BO all sts loosely.

Finishing
Block pieces gently on WS using a warm
iron over a damp cloth. With RS's together,
sew three side seams; turn Cushion RS out.

CUSHION 1
Twisted Cord: Using B, cut 4 lengths of yarn
each approximately 13 feet long, and make a
Twisted Cord (see Special Techniques, page
178). Stitch twisted cord along seam on three
sides of cushion. Stuff with cushion insert; sew
remaining side, leaving a small hole in corner.
Stitch remainder of cord along final side, tucking
end of cord into hole in seam. Stitch to secure.

CUSHION 2
Tassels: Thread loop on tassels through work
at corners; stitch to secure. Stuff with cushion
insert and sew remaining side.

CUSHION 3
Stuff with cushion insert and sew remaining side.

Center

KEY   □ **A**—Knit on RS, purl on WS.   ▣ **B**—Knit on RS, purl on WS.

WARMING UP

Hats, Scarves, Mittens, Gloves, and Socks

Knitting these hats, striped in swirls as colorful as old-fashioned hard candy, is a unique way to get into the holiday spirit. Designer Penney Kolb remembers her mother making similar hats every Christmas for just about everyone: her children, her nephew, the neighborhood kids, and eventually her grandchildren and great-nephews.

FINISHED MEASUREMENTS

To fit Baby (Child, Woman, Man)
Finished hat circumference $16\frac{1}{2}$ ($18\frac{1}{2}$, 21, 23)"

YARN

Mission Falls 1824 Wool (100% wool;
85 yards / 50 grams); 1 (1, 2, 2) skeins
each in 2 colors: A and B
Shown in (see opposite and page 176):
#028 pistachio (green) and #008 earth (brown);
#025 mallow (pink) and # 008 earth (brown);
and #021 denim and #004 charcoal

NEEDLES

One 16" circular (circ) needle size US 6 (4 mm)
One set of five double-pointed needles (dpn)
size US 6 (4 mm)
Change needle size if necessary to obtain
correct gauge.

NOTIONS

Stitch marker, yarn needle

GAUGE

20 sts and 24 rows = 4" (10 cm) in Stockinette
stitch (St st)

candy cane hat

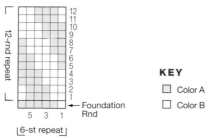

KEY
☐ Color A
☐ Color B

NOTES

❊ **Color pattern** (see Chart)
Foundation Rnd (F): * With B, k1; with A,
k5; repeat from * around.
Rnds 1 and 2: * With B, k2; with A, k3;
with B, k1; repeat from * around.
Rnds 3 and 4: * With B, k3; with A, k3;
repeat from * around.
Rnds 5 and 6: * With A, k1; with B, k3;
with A, k2; repeat from * around.
Rnds 7 and 8: * With A, k2; with B, k3;
with A, k1; repeat from * around.
Rnds 9 and 10: * With A, k3; with B, k3;
repeat from * around.
Rnds 11 and 12: * With B; k1; with A, k3;
with B, k2; repeat from * around.
Repeat Rnds 1–12 for Color pattern.

Hat

Using circ needle and A, CO 84 (96, 108, 114) sts.
Join for working in the rnd, being careful not
to twist sts; place marker (pm) for beginning
of rnd. Begin St st; work even for $1\frac{1}{2}$".
Join B; continuing in St st, begin Color pattern.
Work even until piece measures 5 ($6\frac{1}{4}$, $8\frac{1}{4}$, 9)"
from beginning, end after finishing Rnd 2 or
Rnd 8 of Color pattern.

Crown Shaping

*Note: For remainder of Hat, work A sts using A
and B sts using B; then continue with A only.*
Rnd 1: K1, * skp, k4; repeat from * around.
Rnd 2 and all even rnds: Knit.
Rnd 3: * K3, skp; repeat from * around.
Rnd 5: * K2tog, k2; repeat from * around.
Rnd 7: * K1, k2tog; repeat from * around.
Rnd 8: Knit.
Rnd 9: * K2tog; repeat from * around.
Repeat Rnd 9 until 6 sts remain. Do not
break off yarn.

Finishing

On remaining 6 sts, work 4" of I-cord (see
Special Techniques, page 175). Break yarn
leaving a 4" tail; thread through all sts twice,
then draw tight and fasten off securely.
Weave in ends. Tie I-cord in a knot.

Fur-Trimmed Hood and Gauntlet Gloves

Hoods are often associated with darkness or dark figures, but this one's more urban mystique than goth, lightened up by sophisticated colors and flirtatious details that are repeated in the gauntlet gloves. It's also wonderfully practical—it won't ruin a holiday hairdo, but will keep you warm, whether you're out caroling or braving the cold to meet friends at a neighborhood bistro.

FINISHED MEASUREMENTS
Hood: 10" deep by 13" high from shoulder
Gloves: 7¼" palm circumference

YARN
GGH Maxima (100% merino wool; 121 yards / 50 grams): 4 balls #5 chocolate (MC), 1 ball each #34 rose (A) and #10 dijon (B)
GGH Lara (90% virgin wool / 10% nylon; 60 yards / 50 grams): 1 ball #13 rose (C) for edging

NEEDLES
One 24" circular (circ) needle size US 5 (3.75 mm)
One 24" circular needle size US 6 (4 mm)
One set of five double-pointed needles (dpn) size US 5 (3.75 mm)
One set of five double-pointed needles size US 6 (4 mm)
Two double-pointed needles size US 11 (8 mm) for fur trim
Change needle size if necessary to obtain correct gauge.

NOTIONS
Stitch markers (at least 15, including 5 split-ring markers), yarn needle, waste yarn

GAUGE
22 sts and 23 rows/rnds = 4" (10 cm) in Stockinette stitch (St st) and Colorwork from Chart using larger (size US 6) needles; 22 sts and 28 rows/rnds = 4" (10 cm) in St st using MC and smaller (size US 5) needles

NOTES
⁜ The Hood is worked straight (back and forth in rows) from top to lower edge, on a circular needle, using Stranded method (see Special Techniques, page 177); the extra length of the circ needle is required to keep the colorwork from being stranded too tightly.

⁜ Row 1 of the Hood Colorwork Chart is a WS row; read WS rows from left to right, RS rows from right to left.

⁜ After the rows/rounds in which 3 colors are used in 1 row/round, carry the third color (B) up the side and it will be in the correct position when the pattern changes and it becomes the dominant contrast color.

⁜ The large motifs at the lower edge of the Hood are worked in Intarsia (see Special Techniques, page 175). To make working these motifs manageable, prepare the yarn as follows:
For each color A section, cut a 2-yard length of yarn; for each color B section, cut a 1-yard length of yarn; for each 1-st center, cut a 7" length of A. Begin working each length of yarn from its center, so that you can use one end to work each "arm" of the motif; be sure that your tension is not too tight on the first stitch, because it will be hard to fix after both ends are worked away from it. Carry the MC across the Intarsia sections.

⁜ The gloves are worked in-the-round using dpn; read all rounds of the Colorwork Chart from right to left.

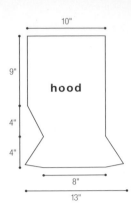

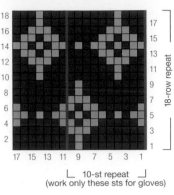

18-row repeat

└ 10-st repeat ┘
(work only these sts for gloves)

KEY

Note: Knit on RS, purl on WS using colors shown

- ■ Chocolate (MC)
- ■ Rose (A)
- ■ Dijon (B)
- ☑ M1-R: Right-slanting make 1
- ☒ M1-L: Left-slanting make 1

Hood

Using smaller circ needle and MC, CO 109 sts (107 pattern sts and 2 selvage sts; work selvage sts in MC throughout). DO NOT JOIN. Change to larger circ needle and begin Colorwork Chart.

Establish Pattern: Using MC, k1 (selvage st); beginning Row 1 of Colorwork Chart, work 53 sts, place marker (pm), work center Back st from chart, pm, work 53 sts from chart, k1 using MC (selvage st). Continue as established until 52 rows of the chart have been worked; piece measures approximately 9".

Decrease Row (RS): Continuing as established, decrease 1 st each side of center back st this row, then every other row 9 more times—89 sts, maintaining existing sts in Colorwork pattern as established. Work 1 row even, removing center Back markers. (Row 18 of Chart has just been completed).

(WS) Change to smaller circ needle and MC only; work 2 rows even in St st.

Next Row (WS): P3, pm, p11, * pm, p1, pm, p11; repeat from * to last 3 sts, pm, p3.

Next Row (RS): Beg Hood Shoulder Chart, working Chart on 11-st sections between the markers; work shaping and colorwork as indicated on the chart.

Work Rows 1–28 of the chart once—145 sts. Continuing with MC only, knit 2 rows even. BO all sts.

Finishing

Block piece to measurements, paying special attention to colorwork areas. Weave in ends, taking care not to distort colorwork with yarn ends.

Graft top of Hood together using MC and Kitchener st (see Special Techniques, page 176).

Fur Trim: Using largest (size US 11) dpn and C, CO 3 sts.

Work applied I-cord as follows: With RS facing, beginning at lower right corner of Hood using the needle with the 3 sts on it, * pick up and knit 1 st between edge st and first pattern st— 4 sts; slide sts to opposite end of needle, k2, k2tog-tbl—3 sts remain. Repeat from *, picking up sts from every other vertical row 4 or 5 times, then every third vertical row once.

Continue until hood opening is edged in fur; cut yarn, leaving an 8" tail, draw yarn through live sts and fasten off.

Weave in ends. Use a needle tip or a hair brush to bring fringe of fur yarn to RS of work.

Twisted Cords: For each cord, cut three 30" lengths, one each MC, A, and B. Work 2 Twisted Cords (see Special Techniques, page 178).

With WS of Hood facing, thread yarns through edge of Hood where the fur edging meets Hood fabric at the neck, so that an equal amount is on either side. Knot ends together so that cord is approximately 10" long and smooth so that twist is evenly distributed; trim ends.

Repeat for other side.

Gauntlet Gloves

Left Glove

Using smallest dpn, MC, and Long-Tail CO method (see Special Techniques, page 176), CO 50 sts; distribute evenly on 4 needles. Join for working in the round, being careful not to twist sts; pm for beginning of rnd. Purl 1 rnd. Change to larger dpn and work Rnds 1–18 of Colorwork Chart once, then Rnds 1–9 once; piece measures approximately 4¾" from the beginning.

Wrist

Rnd 1: Change to smallest dpn; using MC only, * k2tog, k3; repeat from * around— 40 sts remain.
Rnd 2: * K8, k2tog; repeat from * around— 36 sts remain.
Rnd 3: Purl.
Rnd 4: Knit.
Rnds 5–8: Repeat Rnds 3 and 4 [Garter ridges]. Distribute sts evenly on 4 needles.
Rnd 9: K1, M1-R, knit around to last st of second needle, M1-L, k2, M1-R, knit around to last st of fourth needle, M1-L, k1—40 sts.
Rnds 10–13: Knit.

Thumb Gusset and Fingers

Rnd 1: Knit around to last 3 sts of second needle, M1-L, k2, M1-R, knit to end of rnd.
Rnd 2 and all even numbered rnds: Knit even.
Rnd 3: Knit around to last 5 sts of second needle, M1-L, k4, M1-R, knit to end of rnd.
Rnd 5: Knit around to last 7 sts of second needle, M1-L, k6, M1-R, knit to end of rnd.
Rnd 7: Knit around to last 9 sts of second needle, M1-L, k8, M1-R, knit to end of rnd.
Rnd 9: Knit around to last 11 sts of second needle, M1-L, k10, M1-R, knit to end of rnd.
Rnd 11: Knit around to last 13 sts of second needle, M1-L, k12, M1-R, knit to end of rnd.
Rnd 13: Knit around to last 15 sts of second needle, place next 14 sts on a piece of waste yarn, turn; CO 2 sts using Backward Loop CO method (see Special Techniques, page 174), turn; knit to end of rnd—40 sts. Work even in St st until hand measures 3½–4" from Garter ridges on Wrist (glove should come to base of little finger), ending 4 sts before end of rnd.
Little Finger: Place last 4 sts from fourth needle and first 4 sts from first needle on waste yarn, turn; CO 2 sts onto fourth needle using Backward Loop CO method, turn; knit 2 rnds even, ending 6 sts before end of second rnd.

Ring Finger: Place last 6 sts from fourth needle and first 4 sts from first needle on waste yarn for Ring Finger, turn; CO 2 sts onto fourth needle using Backward Loop CO method, turn; knit 2 rnds (you may place work on 3 needles instead of 4, making sure not to disturb beginning/end of rnd), ending 7 sts before end of second rnd.

Middle Finger: Place last 7 sts of rnd and first 5 sts of rnd on waste yarn for Middle Finger.

Index Finger: Turn; CO 2 sts using Backward Loop CO method—16 sts for Index Finger, turn (RS facing); join for working in the rnd. Place split-ring marker at base of Finger; work even for 17 rnds, or to desired length (until only the tip of finger shows).

Next Rnd: * K2tog; repeat from * around. Cut yarn, leaving an 8" tail; draw through live sts, pull tight, and fasten off.

Middle Finger: Place 12 sts from waste yarn on dpn; join new yarn, pick up and knit 2 sts from fourchette (the 2 CO sts at base of Index Finger)—14 sts. PM at base of Finger; work even for 20 rnds, or to desired length. Complete as for Index Finger.

Ring Finger: Place 10 sts from waste yarn on dpn; join new yarn, pick up and knit 2 sts from fourchette—12 sts. PM at base of Finger; work even for 18 rnds, or to desired length. Complete as for Index Finger.

Little Finger: Place 8 sts from waste yarn on dpn; join new yarn, pick up and knit 2 sts from fourchette—10 sts. PM at base of Finger; work even for 16 rnds, or to desired length. Complete as for Index Finger.

Thumb: Place 14 sts from waste yarn on dpn; join new yarn, pick up and knit 2 sts from CO sts on hand—16 sts. PM at base of Thumb; work even for 15 rnds, or to desired length. Complete as for Index Finger.

Right Glove

Work as for left Glove until beginning of thumb gusset shaping.

Thumb Gusset and Fingers

Rnd 1: Knit around to beginning of third needle, k1, M1-L, k2, M1-R, knit to end of rnd.

Rnd 2 and all even numbered rnds: Knit even.

Rnd 3: Knit around to beginning of third needle, k1, M1-L, k4, M1-R, knit to end of rnd.

Rnd 5: Knit around to beginning of third needle, k1, M1-L, k6, M1-R, knit to end of rnd.

Rnd 7: Knit around to beginning of third needle, k1, M1-L, k8, M1-R, knit to end of rnd.

Rnd 9: Knit around to beginning of third needle, k1, M1-L, k10, M1-R, knit to end of rnd.

Rnd 11: Knit around to beginning of third needle, k1, M1-L, k12, M1-R, knit to end of rnd.

Rnd 13: Knit around to beginning of third needle, k1, place next 14 sts on a piece of waste yarn, turn; CO 2 sts using Backward Loop CO method, turn; knit to end of rnd—40 sts. Complete as for Left Glove.

Finishing

Block pieces to measurements, paying special attention to colorwork areas. Weave in ends, taking care not to distort colorwork with yarn ends; use yarn ends at base of fingers to sew up any gaps.

Fur Trim: Beginning at Thumb side for each Glove, work applied I-cord around edge of Glove as for Hood, picking up one st every 2 sts 4 or 5 times, then every 3 sts once.

When the beginning of edging is reached, cut yarn leaving an 8" tail, draw yarn through live sts, then weave through beginning and end of edging to join.

Weave in ends. Use a needle tip or a hair brush to bring fringe of fur yarn to RS of work.

BETTY CHRISTIANSEN *Vintage Beaded Gloves*

These ladylike gloves were inspired by a pair Betty Christiansen found in an antique store in St. Paul, Minnesota. They hark back to the days when women, like her grandmother, didn't leave the house without matching hats and gloves, especially for holiday social occasions. This pair is designed flat, without a gusset, so they look as pretty and ladylike draped in the hand as they are on it. While delicate-looking, the alpaca and silk yarn they are knit with makes them sturdy and warm as well as luxurious. A mock-cable cuff and simple beading add a little holiday dazzle.

FINISHED MEASUREMENTS
To fit: Small (Medium, Large)
7 (7½, 8)" hand circumference

YARN
Blue Sky Alpaca Alpaca & Silk (50% alpaca / 50% silk; 146 yards / 50 grams): 2 balls all sizes Shown in #133 blush with amethyst bugle beads and cream pearls

NEEDLES
One set of five double-pointed needles (dpn) size US 1 (2.25 mm)
Change needle size if necessary to obtain correct gauge.

NOTIONS
Waste yarn, yarn needle, sewing thread, beading needle

BEADS
36 (3 mm) pearl beads, 92 (6 mm) bugle beads (see Sources for Supplies, page 182)

GAUGE
34 sts and 42 rows = 4" (10 cm) in Stockinette stitch (St st)

NOTES
✣ **LT** (Left twist): Knit into the back of the loop of second stitch on left-hand needle, but do not remove st from needle, knit into the front loop of first stitch on left-hand needle, drop both sts from left-hand needle.
✣ **RT** (Right twist): Knit into the front loop of the second stitch on left-hand needle, but do not remove st from needle, knit into the front loop of first st on left-hand needle, drop both sts from left-hand needle.
✣ **Cable Rib** (multiple of 3 sts; 4-rnd repeat)
Rnd 1: * RT, p1; repeat from * around.
Rnd 2: * K2, p1; repeat from * around.
Rnd 3: * LT, p1; repeat from * around.
Rnd 4: * K2, p1; repeat from * around.
Repeat Rnds 1–4 for Cable Rib.
✣ **Twisted Rib** (multiple of 2 sts; 1-rnd repeat)
Every Rnd: * K1-tbl, p1; repeat from * around.

Left Glove

Cuff

CO 90 (96, 102) sts and divide evenly onto 3 dpn. Join for working in the rnd, being careful not to twist sts; place marker (pm) for beginning of rnd.

Work 16 rnds in Cable Rib.

Decrease Rnd: * K2tog, p1; repeat from * around—60 (64, 68) sts remain.

Change to Twisted Rib; work even for 5 rnds.

Change to St st.

Hand

Work even for $2\frac{1}{2}$ ($2\frac{3}{4}$, 3)" (or until Glove reaches the base of your thumb).

Divide for Thumb: K20 (21, 22); place next 10 (11, 12) sts on waste yarn, CO 10 (11, 12) sts; k30 (32, 34).

Continuing in St st, work even until Glove measures $3\frac{1}{4}$ ($3\frac{1}{2}$, $3\frac{3}{4}$)" from Twisted Rib section, (or reaches the base of your Little Finger).

Little Finger

Beginning with Needle 1, k7 (8, 8) sts; place 46 (48, 52) sts on waste yarn; CO 1 st, k7 (8, 8)—15 (17, 17) sts total.

Divide sts evenly on 3 needles, and knit every rnd until Finger measures $1\frac{3}{4}$ (2, $2\frac{1}{4}$)" (or reaches the tip of your pinky).

* K2tog; repeat from * around, ending k1.

Break yarn, thread tail through remaining sts, and fasten off.

Upper Hand

Divide 46 (48, 52) sts from waste yarn evenly onto 3 needles. Join the yarn at the gap between the Little Finger and the rest of the Hand, and pick up 2 sts from the CO edge at the base of the Little Finger—48 (50, 54) sts total. Knit around for $\frac{1}{4}$", being sure to end at the point between the picked-up sts.

Ring Finger

Place 8 (8, 9) sts from the Front and 8 (8, 9) sts from the Back onto 2 needles. Place the remaining 32 (34, 36) sts on waste yarn. Dividing the sts evenly over 3 needles as you work, join yarn, k8 (8, 9), CO 1 st, k8 (8, 9)—17 (17, 19) sts.

Knit every rnd until Finger measures $2\frac{1}{4}$ ($2\frac{1}{2}$, $2\frac{3}{4}$)" (or reaches the tip of your ring finger). Complete as for Little Finger.

Middle Finger

Place 8 (9, 9) sts from the Front and 8 (9, 9) sts from the Back onto 2 needles. Leave the remaining 16 (16, 18) sts on waste yarn. Dividing the sts evenly over 3 needles as you work, join yarn at the gap between the Ring Finger and the Middle Finger, pick up 2 sts from the CO edge at the base of the Ring Finger, then k8 (9, 9), CO 1 st, k8 (9, 9)—19 (21, 21) sts total.

Knit every rnd until Finger measures $2\frac{1}{2}$ ($2\frac{3}{4}$, 3)" (or reaches the tip of your middle finger). Complete as for Little Finger.

Index Finger

Divide the remaining 16 (16, 18) sts from waste yarn onto 3 needles. Join yarn at the gap between the Middle Finger and the Index Finger; pick up 2 sts from the CO edge at the base of the Middle Finger—18 (18, 20) sts total. Knit every rnd until Finger measures $2\frac{1}{4}$ ($2\frac{1}{2}$, $2\frac{3}{4}$)" (or reaches the tip of your Index Finger). Complete as for Little Finger, ending k2tog instead of k1.

Thumb

Place 10 (11, 12) sts from waste yarn onto needle. Join yarn and, dividing sts evenly over 3 needles as you work, knit across these sts, pick up 1 st in space between these sts and CO edge, pick up 10 (11, 12) sts along CO edge, then pick up 1 st in space between CO edge and beginning of rnd—22 (24, 26) sts total.

Knit every rnd until Thumb measures $1\frac{1}{2}$ ($1\frac{3}{4}$, 2)" [or reaches the tip of your thumb].

Next rnd: * K2tog; repeat from * around— 11 (12, 13) sts remain.

Complete as for Little Finger, ending k1 (k0, k1).

Finishing

Weave in loose ends, being particularly careful to close any gaps between fingers neatly. Using the photo as a guide, sew on pearl and bugle beads.

Right Glove

Work as for Left Glove until Divide for Thumb.
Divide for Thumb: Place 10 (11, 12) sts on waste yarn, CO 10 (11, 12) sts, k50 (53, 56). Continue working even in St st until Glove measures 3¼ (3½, 3¾)" from Twisted Rib section (or reaches the base of your little finger).

Little Finger

Beginning with Needle 1, k37 (40, 42); place next 46 (48, 52) sts on waste yarn; divide the remaining 14 (16, 16) sts evenly onto 3 needles, CO 1 st between Little Finger and remainder of hand—15 (17, 17) sts total. Continue as for Left Glove.

Complete Upper Hand, remaining Fingers, and Thumb as for Left Glove.

IRIS SCHREIER
Snowy Triangle Scarf and Hat

Created from a fluffy boucle yarn, this hat and scarf set is beautifully soft and light—like a snowflake itself. Knit in a series of triangular panels that build on each other in a kind of modular construction, the scarf pattern looks deceptively complicated—it's actually very simple, using only garter stitch and knit in one piece from start to finish. The matching hat is knit from the top down and trimmed with equilateral triangles.

FINISHED MEASUREMENTS
Scarf: Approximately 4" wide by 48" long
Hat: Approximately 18" circumference

YARN
Fiesta La Boheme (2-strand yarn: 100% kid mohair and 100% rayon; 290 yards / 8 ounces): 1 skein vanilla makes both Scarf and Hat

NEEDLES
Scarf: One pair straight needles size US 11 (7 mm)
Hat: One set of five double-pointed (dpn) needles size US 9 (5.5 mm)
Change needle size if necessary to obtain correct gauge.

NOTIONS
Stitch marker, yarn needle

GAUGE
Scarf: 16 sts = 4" (10 cm) in Garter stitch using larger needles
Hat: 14 sts = 4" (10 cm) in Stockinette stitch (St st) using smaller needles

Scarf

Loosely CO 16 sts.

First Triangle
Row 1: K1-f/b, k1, turn; slip 1, knit to end of row.
Row 2: K1-f/b, k3, turn; pm, slip 1, knit to end of row.
Row 3: K1-f/b, knit to marker, remove marker, k1, turn; pm, slip 1, knit to end of row.
Repeat Row 3 until all sts have been worked—31 sts.
Knit 1 row, turn.

Second Triangle
Row 1: K1-f/b, skp, turn; slip 1, knit to end of row.
Row 2: K1-f/b, k1, pm, skp, turn; slip 1, knit to end of row.
Row 3: K1-f/b, knit to marker, skp, turn *; slip 1, knit to end of row.
Repeat Row 3 until all sts have been worked, ending last row at * —31 sts.
Continue making triangles by repeating instructions for Second Triangle a total of eight times or to desired length.

Last Triangle
Row 1: K1-f/b, skp, turn; slip 1, knit to end of row.
Row 2: K1-f/b, k1, pm, skp, turn; slip 1, knit to end of row.
Row 3: K1-f/b, knit to marker, skp, turn; slip 1, knit to end of row.
Repeat Row 3 until 15 sts remain unworked (half the total number, less 1 st), and continue as follows:
Row 1: Skp, knit to marker, skp, turn; slip 1, knit to last st, turn [one st left on right-hand needle].
Row 2: Slip 1, pass first st over just slipped st *, knit to marker, skp, turn; slip 1, knit to last st, turn.
Repeat Row 2 until 3 sts remain. Work Row 2 to *, BO last st. Weave in ends.

NEW YEAR WISHES
AROUND THE GLOBE

*Greet friends and neighbors
from other places with a
Happy New Year wish in their
native languages.*

Arabic Antum salimoun

Chinese Xin nian kuai le

Czech Scastny novy rok

Danish Godt nytår

Dutch Gelukkige nieuwjaar

French Bonne année

German Frohes neues jahr

Greek Eutychismenos ho
kainourgios chronos

Hebrew Shanah tovah

Hindi Nahi varsh ka
shub kamna

Italian Buon anno

Japanese Akemashite omedeto

Korean Laimingu najuju metu

Norwegian Godt nytt år

Polish Nowego roku

Russian Schastlivogo
novogo goda

Spanish Feliz año nuevo

Swedish Gott nytt år

Turkish Mutlu yilbasi

Hat

CO 6 sts, alternating onto 2 dpn as follows:
CO first st on first dpn, CO second st on second dpn, CO third st on first dpn, CO fourth st
on second dpn, CO fifth st on first dpn, and CO
sixth st on second dpn [3 sts on each of 2 dpn].
K1-f/b of each st around—12 sts. Divide sts
evenly on 3 dpn. Join for working in the rnd; pm
for beginning of rnd.
Rnd 1 and all odd-numbered rounds: Knit.
Rnd 2: * K1-f/b, k1; repeat from * around—
18 sts.
Rnd 4: * K1-f/b, k2; repeat from * around—
24 sts.
Rnd 6: * K1-f/b, k3; repeat from * around—
30 sts.
Rnd 8: * K1-f/b, k4; repeat from * around—
36 sts.
Rnd 10: * K1-f/b, k5; repeat from * around—
42 sts.
Rnd 12: * K1-f/b, k6; repeat from * around—
48 sts.
Rnd 14: * K1-f/b, k7; repeat from * around—
54 sts.
Knit even until Hat measures approximately 6"
from beginning.
Decrease rnd: * K2tog, k4; repeat from *
around—45 sts.

Triangle 1
Row 1: K1-f/b, turn; slip 1, turn.
Row 2: K1-f/b, k1, turn; slip 1, k1, turn.
Row 3: K1-f/b, k2, turn; slip 1, k2, turn.
Row 4: K1-f/b, k3, turn; slip 1, k3, turn.
Row 5: K1-f/b, k4, turn; slip 1, k4, turn.
Row 6: K1-f/b, k5, turn; slip 1, k5, turn.
Row 7: K1-f/b, k6, turn; slip 1, k6, turn.
Row 8: K1-f/b, k7, turn; slip 1, k7, turn.
Row 9: K1-f/b, k8, turn; slip 1, k8, turn.
Row 10: K1-f/b, k9, turn; slip 1, k9, turn.
Row 11: K1-f/b, k10, turn; slip 1, k10, turn.
Row 12: K1-f/b, k11, turn; slip 1, k11, turn.
Row 13: K1-f/b, k12, turn; slip 1, k12, turn.
Row 14: K1-f/b, k13, turn; slip 1, k13, turn.
Row 15: K1-f/b, k14, turn; slip 1, k14, turn.

Triangle 2 (with RS facing you)
Row 1: K1-f/b, skp, turn; slip 1, k2, turn.
Row 2: K1-f/b, k1, skp, turn; slip 1, k3, turn.
Row 3: K1-f/b, k2, skp, turn; slip 1, k4, turn.
Row 4: K1-f/b, k3, skp, turn; slip 1, k5, turn.
Row 5: K1-f/b, k4, skp, turn; slip 1, k6, turn.
Row 6: K1-f/b, k5, skp, turn; slip 1, k7, turn.
Row 7: K1-f/b, k6, skp, turn; slip 1, k8, turn.
Row 8: K1-f/b, k7, skp, turn; slip 1, k9, turn.
Row 9: K1-f/b, k8, skp, turn; slip 1, k10, turn.
Row 10: K1 f/b, k9, skp, turn; slip 1, k11, turn.
Row 11: K1-f/b, k10, skp, turn; slip 1,
k12, turn.
Row 12: K1-f/b, k11, skp, turn; slip 1, k13, turn.
Row 13: K1-f/b, k12, skp; do not turn.

Triangle 3 (with RS facing you)
Row 1: K1, turn; skp, turn.
Row 2: Slip 1, k1, turn; slip 1, skp, turn.
Row 3: Slip 1, k2, turn; slip 1, k1, skp, turn.
Row 4: Slip 1, k3, turn; slip 1, k2, skp, turn.
Row 5: Slip 1, k4, turn; slip 1, k3, skp, turn.
Row 6: Slip 1, k5, turn; slip 1, k4, skp, turn.
Row 7: Slip 1, k6, turn; slip 1, k5, skp, turn.
Row 8: Slip 1, k7, turn; slip 1, k6, skp, turn.
Row 9: Slip 1, k8, turn; slip 1, k7, skp, turn.
Row 10: Slip 1, k9, turn; slip 1, k8, skp, turn.
Row 11: Slip 1, k10, turn; slip 1, k9, skp, turn.
Row 12: Slip 1, k11, turn; slip 1, k10, skp, turn.
Row 13: Slip 1, k12, turn; slip 1, k11, skp, turn.
Row 14: Slip 1, k13, turn; slip 1, k12, skp, turn.
Row 15: Slip 1, k14, turn; slip 1, k13, skp, turn.

Triangle 4: Work as Triangle 2
Triangle 5: Work as Triangle 3
Triangle 6: Work as Triangle 2; turn, slip 1,
knit to end of row.
You will have 15 live sts from Triangle 6 and
15 live sts from Triangle 1. Turn the hat inside
out, and using 3-Needle BO (see Special
Techniques, page 177), join the two sets
of sts. Weave in ends.

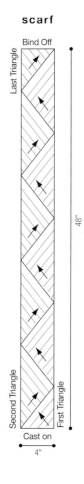

scarf

Bind Off

Last Triangle

Second Triangle

First Triangle

Cast on

4"

48"

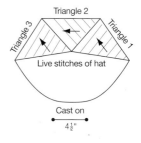

hat

Note: Triangles 4, 5, and 6 are
continued around back.

Triangle 3

Triangle 2

Triangle 1

Live stitches of hat

Cast on

4 1/8"

IRIS SCHREIER

Stained Glass Scarf

The colors and stitch pattern of this reversible scarf combine to create the look of stained glass. A clever technique known as double knitting, in which two right-sided layers are created at once, forms the reversible stained-glass effect and results in a double-thick fabric that offers extra protection in bitter weather. Two methods for double knitting are explained here: two-stranded and slip and slide. The two-stranded method is faster because you complete an entire row with each pass, but it takes a little longer to master. The slip-and-slide method uses only one color at a time, and is recommended for beginners.

FINISHED MEASUREMENTS
Approximately 6½" wide by 60" long

YARNS
Artyarns Ultramerino 6 (100% merino wool; 137 yards / 50 grams): 2 skeins #3113 brown (A)
Artyarns Ultramerino 4 (100% merino wool; 191 yards / 50 grams): 2 skeins #4105 variegated (B)

NEEDLES
One pair straight needles size US 5 (3.75 mm) for two-stranded method
OR
One 16" circular (circ) needle size US 5 (3.75 mm) for slip-and-slide method
Change needle size if necessary to obtain correct gauge.

GAUGE
18 sts and 26 rows = 4" (10 cm) in Scarf Trim Stitch pattern

NOTES
✳ **K1 AB**: Knit 1 stitch using both colors, AB together

Scarf

Choose one of the methods below to continue.

TWO-STRANDED METHOD
For all knit stitches, carry both colors in the same hand, taking both strands to the back when knitting and both to the front when purling. For all purl stitches, separate the strands with one in the front and the other in the back, keeping strand to be purled in front of the needle and the strand to be knit in back. Make sure the strands are not twisted.
Using A, CO 33 sts.
Set-Up Row: Join B; k1 AB, [k1 A and p1 B into the same stitch] 3 times, * [p1 B and k1 A into the same stitch] once, [k1 A and p1 B into the same stitch] 3 times; repeat from * to last st, k1 AB—64 sts.

Scarf Trim
Row 1: K1 AB, [k1 B, p1 A] 3 times, * [p1 A, k1 B] once, [k1 B, p1 A] 3 times; repeat from * to last st, k1 AB—64 sts.
Row 2: K1 AB, [k1 A, p1 B] 3 times, * [p1 B, k1 A] once, [k1 A and p1 B] 3 times; repeat from * to last st, k1 AB.
Note: You will be knitting and purling all stitches as they face you, working each stitch individually except for the first and last stitches of each row where 2 strands are used together. Repeat Rows 1 and 2 a total of 9 times.

Scarf Body (reverse colors)
Row 1: K1 AB, [k1 A and p1 B] 3 times, * [p1 B, k1 A] once, [k1 A, p1 B] 3 times; repeat from * to last st, k1 AB.
Row 2: K1 AB, [k1 B, p1 A] 3 times, * [p1 A, k1 B] once, [k1 B, p1 A] 3 times; repeat from * to last st, k1 AB.
Repeat Rows 1 and 2 until piece measures approximately 54" or desired length.
Repeat Rows 1 and 2 of Scarf Trim 9 times.
BO with A as follows: K1, [ssk, BO one st] 3 times, * p2tog, BO one st, [ssk, BO one st] 3 times; repeat from * to last st, k1, BO last st.
Weave in ends.

This method works one color at a time. A single row is completed in 2 passes, once with each color. A circular needle is required because you will need to slide the stitches into position for knitting the second pass.

With A, CO 64 sts.

Scarf Trim

Row 1: Join B. K1 AB; working with A only, [K1, slip 1 wyif] 3 times, *[k1, slip 1 wyib] once, [k1, slip 1 wyif] 3 times; repeat from * to last st, slip 1 AB. Slide sts to other end of needle.

Row 2: Slip AB wyib; working with B only, [slip 1 wyib, p1] 3 times, *[slip 1 wyif, p1] once, [slip 1 wyib, p1] 3 times; repeat from * to last st, k1 AB. Turn work.

Row 3: K1 AB; working with B only, [k1, slip 1 wyif] 3 times, *[k1, slip 1 wyib] once, [k1, slip 1 wyif] 3 times; repeat from * to last st, slip AB. Slide sts to other end of needle.

Row 4: Slip AB wyib; working with A only, [slip 1 wyib, p1] 3 times, *[slip 1 wyif, p1] once, [slip 1 wyib, p1] 3 times; repeat from * to last st; k1 AB. Turn work.

Work Rows 1–4 a total of 9 times.

Scarf Body (reverse colors)

Row 1: K1 AB; working with B only, [K1, slip 1 wyif] 3 times, *[k1, slip 1 wyib] once, [k1, slip 1 wyif] 3 times; repeat from * to last st, slip 1 AB. Slide sts to other end of needle.

Row 2: Slip 1 AB wyib; working with A only, [slip 1 wyib, p1] 3 times, *[slip 1 wyif, p1] once, [slip 1 wyib, p1] 3 times; repeat from * to last st, k1 AB. Turn work.

Row 3: K1 AB; working with A only, [K1, slip 1 wyif] 3 times, *[k1, slip 1 wyib] once, [k1, slip wyif] 3 times; repeat from * to last st, slip 1 AB. Slide sts to other end of needle.

Row 4: Slip 1 AB wyib; working with B only, [slip 1 wyib, p1] 3 times, *[slip 1 wyif, p1] once, [slip 1 wyib, p1] 3 times; repeat from * to last st, k1 AB. Turn work.

Repeat Rows 1–4 until piece measures approximately 54" or desired length, ending with Row 4 of Stitch pattern. Repeat Rows 1–4 of Scarf Trim a total of 9 times.

BO using A as follows: K1, [ssk, BO one st] 3 times, * p2tog, BO one st, [ssk, BO one st] 3 times; repeat from * to last st, k1, BO last st. Weave in ends.

In colonial America, long stockings that extended over the knee were a staple of a man's wardrobe. Not so here. Cindy Taylor's pair is decidedly feminine in its details— a mock-cable heel flap, a form-fitting shape, and most notably an eyelet cable "seam" up the back (see page 85), reminiscent of old-fashioned silk stockings. A funky, fun alternative to leg warmers, these stockings are a great way to keep cozy under a holiday skirt, or to add an extra layer when taking the dog for a walk. A unique blend of merino wool and linen gives them a beautiful natural color and ensures they're as strong as they are soft.

FINISHED MEASUREMENTS
$19\frac{1}{2}$" from back of heel to top of thigh
$12\frac{3}{4}$" from back of heel to high of toe

YARN
Haneke Exotics (65% merino wool / 35% linen; 164 yards / 1.75 ounces): 4 skeins #10 beige

NEEDLES
One set of five double-pointed needles (dpn) size US 3 (3.25 mm)
Change needle size if necessary to obtain correct gauge.

NOTIONS
Three stitch markers (2 a different color than the third), 2 stitch holders, cable needle, yarn needle

GAUGE
28 sts and 32 rows = 4" (10 cm) in Stockinette stitch (St st)

Sock

Top
CO 84 sts and divide evenly onto 4 dpn. Join for working in the rnd, being careful not to twist sts; pm for beginning of rnd. Begin St st; work even until piece measures 2" from the beginning.

Ribbing
Rnd 1: * P1, k2; repeat from * around.
Rnd 2: * P1, RT; repeat from * around.
Work Rnds 1 and 2 a total of 5 times—10 rnds.

Thigh
Note: Use different colored markers than beginning of rnd marker for next rnd; beginning of rnd marker will be between the 2 new markers, at the center of the 6 sts worked in Lace Cable pattern.
Rearrange needles while working Rnd 1 of Lace Cable pattern as follows: Needle 1—K8, pm, k6 [Rnd 1 of Lace Cable pattern], pm, k8; Needle 2 —K21; Needle 3—K20; Needle 4—K21.
Establish Pattern: Work in St st to marker; work Rnd 2 of Lace Cable from Chart across next 6 sts; work in St st around. Cont as established, working Rnds 3–10 of Lace Cable, then repeat Rnds 1–10 on 6 sts between markers, working remaining sts in St st, and AT THE SAME TIME,
Shape Thigh: Decrease 1 st at each side of Lace Cable every 14 rnds 5 times, working decreases invisibly into the designated pattern rnd as follows:
Note: Move markers and rearrange sts on needles as needed.
To decrease on:
Rnd 2 of pattern: Work to last 2 sts of rnd, slip 2 sts to cn and hold in back; ssk, k2tog from cn.
Rnd 4: Work to last 4 sts of rnd, k3tog, yo twice, sssk.
Rnd 6: Work to last 4 sts of rnd, k3tog, yo, k2, yo, sssk.
Rnd 8: Work to last 4 sts of rnd, k2tog, k4, ssk.
Rnd 10: Work to last 3 sts of rnd, slip 1 st to cn and hold in front, k2tog, k1 from cn; slip next 2 sts to cn and hold in back, k1, ssk from cn.
Rnd 70—last Decrease Rnd: 74 sts remain.
Continuing as established, work even for 25 rnds, ending with Rnd 5 of Lace Cable—95 rnds completed.

Calf

Decrease 1 st at each side of Lace Cable, as above, on next and every following sixth rnd 10 times total, ending with Rnd 10 of Lace Cable pattern—54 sts remain; 150 rnds completed.

Back of Ankle

Knit 1 rnd, rearranging needles as follows: Knit to center of lace cable pattern [new beginning of rnd]; Needle 1—k10; Needles 2 and 3—k17 sts each; with Needle 4, begin ankle Chart, Rnd 1 as follows: K8 (2 sts remaining on Needle 4), RT; slip beginning of rnd marker, work remainder of Chart across Needle 1. Continuing as established on Needles 2 and 3, work Rnds 2–10 of Ankle Chart on Needles 4 and 1, ending 12 sts before end of rnd on Rnd 10 (2 sts remaining unworked on Needle 3). Slip last 2 unworked sts of Needle 3 onto Needle 4, and the first 2 sts of Needle 2 onto the end of Needle 1—12 sts each on Needles 4 and 1—24 sts total for Heel Flap. Place sts from Needles 2 and 3 on holder(s) for Instep to be worked later.

Heel Flap

Using a spare needle, work across 24 sts from Needles 4 and 1 as follows: (RS) M1, work 24 sts in Heel pattern (as for Rnd 9 of chart), M1—26 Heel sts. Continue working back and forth on Heel sts in Heel pattern as follows:
Row 1 (WS): Slip 1, purl across.
Row 2: Slip 1, (RT) to last st, k1.
Repeat these 2 rows 7 more times, repeat Row 1 once more—17 rows.

LACE CABLE CHART

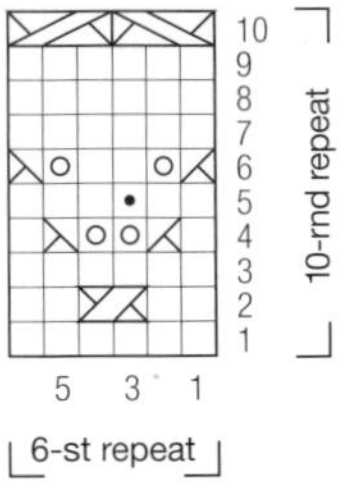

10
9
8
7
6
5
4
3
2
1

10-rnd repeat

5   3   1

| 6-st repeat |

ANKLE CHART

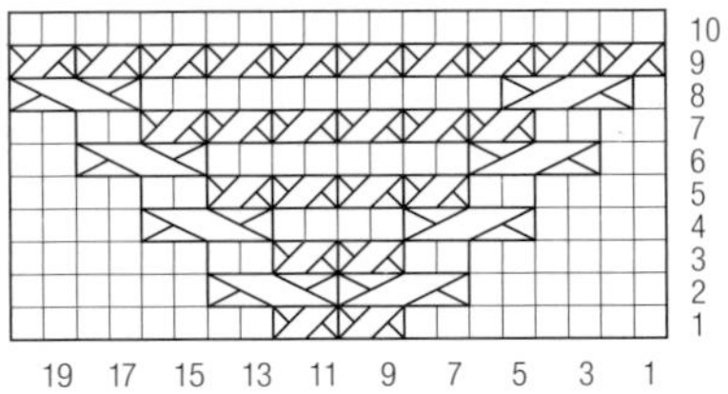

10
9
8
7
6
5
4
3
2
1

19 17 15 13 11 9   7   5   3   1

KEY

☐ Knit on RS, purl on WS

⊡ Purl on RS, knit on WS

⊙ Yo

⧄ K2tog

⧅ Ssk

RT: Knit into the front loop of the second st on left-hand needle, but do not remove st from needle, knit into the front loop of first st on left-hand needle, drop both sts from left-hand needle.

Slip 2 sts to cn, hold to back, k1, k2 fron cn.

Slip next st to cn, hold to front, k2, k1 from cn.

Slip 2 sts to cn, hold to back, k2, k2 from cn.

Slip 2 sts to cn, hold to front, k2, k2 from cn.

Turn Heel

Work Short Rows as follows:

Rows 1 (RS) and 2 (WS): K15, skp, k1, turn; slip 1, p5, p2tog, p1, turn.

Rows 3 and 4: Slip 1, k6, skp, k1, turn; slip 1, p7, p2tog, p1, turn.

Rows 5 and 6: Slip 1, k8, skp, k1, turn; slip 1, p9, p2tog, p1, turn.

Rows 7 and 8: Slip 1, k10, skp, k1, turn; slip 1, p11, p2tog, p1, turn.

Rows 9 and 10: Slip 1, k12, skp, k1, turn; slip 1, p13, p2tog, p1, turn—16 sts remain.

Row 11: K8, pm for beginning of rnd.

Gussets

With Needle 1, knit remaining 8 Heel sts, then pick up and knit 12 sts along side of Heel Flap; work across Needles 2 and 3; with Needle 4, pick up and knit 12 sts along other side of Heel Flap, knit across 8 Heel sts to beginning of rnd—70 sts.

Decrease rnd: Needle 1—Knit across to last 3 sts, k2tog, k1; work across Needles 2 and 3; Needle 4—k1, skp, knit to end of rnd.

Work 1 rnd even.

Repeat decrease rnd every other rnd until 56 sts remain.

Foot

Work even in St st until foot measures 7¾" from back of Heel, or 2" less than desired length.

Toe

Rearrange sts, without changing the beginning of rnd, so that there are 14 sts on each needle.

Decrease rnd: * Needle 1—Knit across to last 3 sts, k2tog, k1; Needle 2—k1, skp, knit to end of needle; repeat from * for Needles 3 and 4.

Work 1 rnd even.

Repeat Decrease rnd every other rnd until 24 sts remain. Using Needle 4, knit sts from Needle 1; slip Needle 3 sts onto Needle 2. Graft sts together using Kitchener st (see Special Techniques, page 176). Weave in ends.

JO SHARP *Holly Leg Warmers*

Before venturing out to choose this year's Christmas tree—whether you cut it yourself in the woods or drag it home from the corner market down city streets—pull on these leg warmers for some added warmth and holiday spirit. Bright and festive, the traditional Christmas colors and patterned stripes are a sure way to bring on the holiday cheer at the beginning of the season. Look closely at the Fair Isle patterning, and you'll find it forms garlands of holly leaves.

FINISHED MEASUREMENTS
Approximately 15" circumference after seaming by 20" long

YARN
Jo Sharp Classic DK Wool Heather (100% wool; 107 yards / 50 grams): 1 ball #907 scarlet (A), 2 balls #912 brocade (B), 1 skein each #803 lichen (C), #903 silk (D), #908 glade (E), #911 maple (F)

NEEDLES
One pair straight needles size US 5 (3.75 mm)
One pair straight needles size US 6 (4.00 mm)
Change needle sizes if necessary to obtain correct gauge.

GAUGE
25 sts and 25 rows = 4" (10 cm) in Fair Isle pattern using larger needles.

Leg Warmer (make 2)

Using smaller needles and A, CO 100 sts; begin k2, p2 rib.
Work even until piece measures 3" from the beginning, ending with a WS row.

Change to larger needles and St st; begin Chart. Carrying color not in use loosely across WS, work 10-st repeat of pattern 10 times across; work Rows 1–22 a total of 4 times— 88 rows.

Change to smaller needles, A, and k2, p2 rib; work even for 3". BO all sts in rib.

Finishing
Block gently on WS using a warm iron over a damp cloth. With RS's together, fold in half lengthwise. Sew side seams to form a tube.

FAIR ISLE CHART

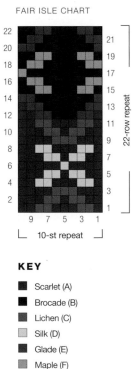

KEY

■ Scarlet (A)
■ Brocade (B)
■ Lichen (C)
□ Silk (D)
■ Glade (E)
■ Maple (F)

ROBIN MELANSON
Nutcracker Slippers

Some knitted slippers are—let's face it—not exactly flattering. But Robin Melanson has broken with tradition by designing these based on the classic leather ballet-slipper style. Delicate and feminine, they are pretty on the foot as well as comfortable and quick to make.

SIZES
Small (Medium, Large)
To fit US women's shoe size 6–6½ (7–7½, 8–8½); average width. Shown in size Medium.

FINISHED MEASUREMENTS
8 (8½, 9)" long

YARN
Rowan Yorkshire Tweed 4-Ply (100% wool; 120 yards / 25 grams): 2 balls #278 bristle (MC), 1 ball #274 brilliant (CC)

NEEDLES
One pair straight needles size US 2 (3 mm)
One set of five double-pointed (dpn) needles size US 2 (3 mm)
Change needle size if necessary to obtain correct gauge.

NOTIONS
Stitch markers, yarn needle

GAUGE
27 sts and 40 rows = 4" (10 cm) in Stockinette stitch (St st)

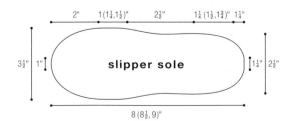

2" 1 (1¼,1½)" 2½" 1¼ (1½,1¾)" 1¼"

3½" 1" slipper sole 1¼" 2½"

8 (8½, 9)"

NOTES
✣ Slippers are both alike, and stretch slightly to fit.
✣ Sole is worked flat; Upper is picked up from the edge of the Sole and worked in-the-round.

Slipper

Sole (make 2)
Using straight needles, MC, and Long-Tail CO method (see Special Techniques, page 176), CO 9 sts.
(WS) Purl 1 row even.
Shape Heel: Increase 1 st each side this row, then every other row 3 times—17 sts.
Work even until piece measures 1¼" from beginning; place marker (pm) each side of row. Continue as established until piece measures 2½ (2¾, 3)" from beginning; pm each side of row.
Shape Foot: Increase 1 st each side this row, then every 12 rows twice—23 sts.
Work even until piece measures 5 (5¼, 5½)" from the beginning; pm each side of row. Continue as established until piece measures 6 (6½, 7)" from the beginning; pm each side of row.
Shape Toe: Decrease 1 st each side this row, every 4 rows 3 times, then every other row 4 times—7 sts remain; piece measures 8 (8½, 9)" from beginning.
Block Sole to measurements shown in diagram before adding Upper.

Upper
Mark center Heel and center Toe on Sole. With RS facing, using dpn and MC, pick up and knit 12 sts from center of Heel to first marker, 8 (10, 12) sts to second marker, 18 sts to third marker, 7 (8, 9) sts to fourth marker, 18 sts to center of Toe, pm; pick up and knit center Toe st, then distribute sts on 2 dpn for one side of upper. Using a new needle, pick up and knit 18 sts from center Toe to fifth marker, 7 (8, 9) sts to sixth marker, 18 sts to seventh marker, 8 (10, 12) sts to eighth marker, 12 sts to center Heel, pm; pick up and knit 1 st for center Back Heel, then distribute sts for other side of Upper on 2 needles—64 (67, 70) sts each side; 128 (134, 140) sts total. Remove all markers EXCEPT center Toe and center Heel (end of rnd).

Next Rnd: K6, pm; knit to last 7 sts, pm; knit to end of rnd.

Knit 4 rnds even.

Shape Upper: Slipping markers as you come to them, knit to 2 sts before first marker, k2tog; ssk, knit around past center Toe marker, ending 2 sts before third marker, k2tog; ssk, knit to end of rnd—4 sts decreased.

Repeat decrease rnd every other rnd 4 more times—108 (114, 120) sts remain. Knit 1 rnd even.

Point pattern

Rnd 1: K20 (22, 24), yo, k1, yo, k15 (16, 17), yo, k1, yo, k15, dcd, move center marker; k15, yo, k1, yo, k15 (16, 17), yo, k1, yo, k20 (22, 24), yo, k1, yo (last yo occurs at end of rnd, take care not to lose it when beg next rnd)— 116 (122, 128) sts.

Rnds 2 and 4: Knit.

Rnd 3: K20 (22, 24), yo, k3, yo, k15 (16, 17), yo, k3, yo, k14, dcd, k14, yo, k3, yo, k15 (16, 17), yo, k3, yo, k20 (22, 24), yo, k3, yo— 124 (130, 136) sts.

Change to CC.

Rnd 5: K21 (23, 25), k2tog, yo, k18 (19, 20), k2tog, yo, k15, dcd, k14, k2tog, yo, k18 (19, 20), k2tog, yo, k23 (25, 27), k2tog, yo, k2— 122 (128, 134) sts.

BO all sts.

Laces (make 2)

Using dpn and CC, CO 3 sts; work I-cord (see Special Techniques, page 175) 60" long, slightly stretched.

Finishing

Lightly steam edge where Sole meets Upper. Weave in ends. Thread laces through the eyelets created on the last round of knitting, crossing laces over ankle to Back of Heel, where both laces go through one eyelet; wind Laces around ankle before tying.

These warm, soft, his-and-her socks are ideal for romantic evenings by the fire. They'd make as heartfelt a gift for newlyweds as they would for a long-committed pair celebrating a landmark holiday season together. Although the two yarns with which they are made differ in fiber content, weight, and construction, they look similar, as though they belong together, just as many couples do after spending many years sharing their lives.

SIZES
To fit US shoe sizes: Woman's $7\frac{1}{2}$–$8\frac{1}{2}$
(Woman's $9\frac{1}{2}$–Man's $8\frac{1}{2}$)

FINISHED MEASUREMENTS
Leg length: $7\frac{1}{2}$ (8)"
Foot circumference: $7\frac{1}{2}$ (8)"

YARN
Rowan Cork (90% merino / 10% nylon;
120 yards / 50 grams): 3 skeins #SH003
for woman's sock
Cascade Pastaza (50% llama / 50% wool;
132 yards / 100 grams): 3 skeins #026
for man's sock

NEEDLES
Woman's: One set of five double-pointed
needles (dpn) size US 5 (3.75 mm)
Man's: One set of five double-pointed needles
size US 6 (4 mm)
Change needle size if necessary to obtain
correct gauge.

NOTIONS
Cable needle, yarn needle

GAUGE
24 sts and 28 rnds (20 sts and 24 rnds) = 4"
(10 cm) in Stockinette stitch (St st) using
smaller (larger) needles

Sock

Leg
Using appropriate yarn and needle size, CO 48 (56) sts; divide evenly over 4 needles. Join for working in the rnd, being careful not to twist sts; place marker (pm) for beginning of rnd [this is the side of the sock]. Begin k2, p2 ribbing Chart; work 24-st repeat between red lines for woman's sock (28-st repeat for man's sock) until piece measures 2 ($2\frac{1}{4}$)" from the beginning. Change to Cable Chart; work 42 (36) rows following Cable Chart, ending with Row 6 (36) of Chart.

Heel
Work 24 (28) sts in Cable pattern onto one needle for heel, changing first and last purl st to knit for woman's size; place remaining 24 (28) Instep sts on a holder to be worked later. Working back and forth in rows [work odd numbered rows as RS rows, even numbered rows as WS rows] on Heel sts only, slipping the first st of each row purlwise, continue from Chart, ending with WS Row 28 (22).

Turn heel
Set-up Row 1: (RS) K14 (16), ssk, k1, turn.
Set-up Row 2: (WS) Slip 1, p5, p2tog, p1, turn.
Continue as follows:
Row 1: Slip 1, knit to 1 st before gap, ssk [the 2 sts on either side of gap], k1, turn.
Row 2: Slip 1, purl to 1 st before gap, p2tog [the 2 sts on either side of gap], p1, turn.
Repeat Rows 1 and 2 three (four) times, omitting the final k1 and p1 sts in the last repeat of Row 2—14 (16) sts remain.

Gusset and Foot

Using the first needle, work across Heel sts, then with the same needle, pick up and knit 11 (11) sts along the left side of Heel flap; using the second and third needles, work across the Instep sts in pattern as established [Rnd 7 (1) of Chart]; using the fourth needle, pick up and knit 11 (11) sts along the right side of Heel flap, then with the same needle, k7 (8); pm for new beginning of rnd—60 (66) sts.

Decrease Rnd: On first needle, work across to last 3 sts, k2tog, k1; continue as established on second and third needles; at beginning of fourth needle, k1, ssk, knit to end. Work 1 rnd even Work Decrease rnd every other rnd (on even numbered rnds), until 12 (14) sts remain on each needle—48 (56) sts. Working in St st on sole, continue in Cable pattern on Instep sts, until foot measures $7\frac{1}{2}$ ($7\frac{1}{2}$)" or $2\frac{1}{2}$ (3)" less than desired finished length.

Knit even for 2 rnds on all sts.

Toe

Decrease Rnd: * On first needle, knit across to last 3 sts, k2tog, k1; on second needle, k1, ssk, knit to end; repeat from * on third and fourth needles. Knit 1 rnd even.

Work Decrease rnd every other rnd until 24 (32) sts remain, then every rnd until 8 sts remain. Knit to end of Needle 1.

Break off yarn leaving a 10" tail. Graft sts together using Kitchener st (see Special Techniques, page 176). Weave in ends. Block on sock blockers or under a damp towel.

CABLE CHART

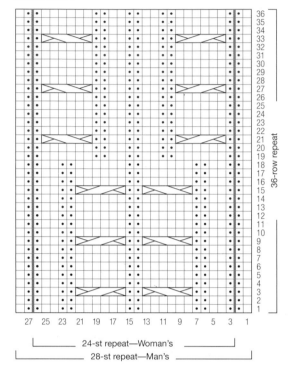

36-row repeat

24-st repeat—Woman's
28-st repeat—Man's

K2, P2 RIBBING CHART

Repeat

24-st repeat—Woman's
28-st repeat—Man's

KEY

☐ Knit on RS, purl on WS.

⊡ Purl on RS, knit on WS.

Sl 3 sts to cn, hold to back, k3, k3 from cn.

Sl 3 sts to cn, hold to front, k3, k3 from cn.

SUSAN ALAIN
Community Afghan

Winter holidays are a time of generosity—a time of sharing not only with those who mean the most to us, but also with those less fortunate. In some European countries, old traditions call for lighting candles in windows to invite in the wandering and hungry, and some historians believe that folks in Britain and Canada honor Boxing Day, December 26, as the day parish church alms boxes were opened for the poor.

The blanket featured here—ideal for a group to knit for a needy family or to raffle off as a fundraiser—is composed of 96 squares and is worked in simple garter stitch. The squares are portable and don't take long to make; arranging them into the final design is fun and satisfying. Try assembling squares so like-colored corners form triangles along the border (as shown here), place them to form solid-color squares, or let chaos reign and fashion them into a crazy quilt.

FINISHED MEASUREMENTS
Approximately 40" wide by 60" long

MATERIALS
Harrisville Highland Style (100% wool; 200 yards / 100 grams): 2 skeins each #17 Bermuda blue, #7 tundra (gold/green), #8 hemlock (mossy green), #23 magenta, #4 gold, #48 dove gray, #13 peacock (turquoise), #40 topaz (rusty orange), and #18 aubergine (dark purple)
Note: If using stash yarn, approximately 2200 yards worsted-weight yarn in several different colors are needed.

NEEDLES
One pair straight needles size US 7 (4.5 mm)
Crochet hook size US 6/G (4.5 mm) for edging
Change needle size if necessary to obtain correct gauge.

GAUGE
1 square = 5" (12.6 cm)

NOTES
✳ When changing colors, choose a new color with high contrast to the last, especially for the wide stripes across the center of each square.
✳ Stitch count will be the same as the row number through Row 30.

Afghan Squares

Row 1: Using color of choice, CO 1 st.
Row 2—Increase Row: YO, k1—2 sts.
Rows 3–14: YO, knit to end—14 sts.
Row 15: Change color as follows: YO, k3; using both the old and new colors held together, k4; break off old color; knit to end with new color—15 sts.
Row 16: YO, knit to end—16 sts.
Row 17: Repeat Row 15—17 sts.
Rows 18–19: YO, knit to end—19 sts after Row 19.
Row 20: Repeat Row 15—20 sts.
Row 21: YO, knit to end—21 sts.
Row 22: Repeat Row 15—22 sts.
Rows 23–29: YO, knit to end—29 sts after Row 29.
Row 30: Repeat Row 15—30 sts.
Row 31—Decrease Row: Skp, knit to end—29 sts remain.
Rows 32–37: Skp, knit to end—23 sts remain after Row 37.
Row 38: Change color as follows: Skp, knit 3; using both the old and new colors held together, k4; break off old color; knit to end with new color—22 sts remain.
Row 39: Skp, knit to end—21 sts remain.
Row 40: Repeat Row 38—20 sts remain.
Rows 41–42: Skp, knit to end—18 sts remain after Row 42.
Row 43: Repeat Row 38—17 sts remain.
Row 44: Skp, knit to end—16 sts remain.
Row 45: Repeat Row 38—15 sts remain.
Rows 46–59: Skp, knit to end—1 st remains after Row 59.
Break yarn and pull through last stitch to secure, leaving a 12" tail.
Repeat Rows 1–59 until 96 squares are completed.
Pull all ends to the WS of each square (whichever side you choose), and weave them in.

Finishing
When assembling blanket, arrange squares in a rectangle 8 squares wide by 12 squares long on a spread-out bed sheet; roll up sheet when desired arrangement has been achieved. This will hold squares in place until they can be whipstitched together, which can be done by unrolling the sheet to expose one row of squares at a time. Using the tails left over from securing the last loop, sew squares together. Using crochet hook and color of choice, work 2 rows single crochet around entire Afghan.

JO SHARP *Color and Texture Afghan*

This warm, soft afghan might lure you to settle your head for "a long winter's nap," as the poem goes. It works up quickly with large needles in simple garter stitch, making it a great gift that even a beginning knitter can handle.

FINISHED MEASUREMENTS
Approximately 30" wide by 60" long, before adding fringe

YARN
Jo Sharp Silkroad Aran Tweed (85% merino wool / 10% silk / 5% cashmere; 93 yards / 50 grams): 9 balls #124 jewel (A)
Jo Sharp Rare Comfort Infusion Kid Mohair (80% kid mohair / 15% polyamid / 5% wool; 95 yards / 25 grams): 3 balls #613 chamomile (B), and 3 balls #606 swamp (C)

NEEDLES
One 32" circular (circ) needle size US 9 (5.5 mm)
Change needle size if necessary to obtain correct gauge.

NOTIONS
Crochet hook size US 10/J (6 mm) for fringe
Yarn needle

GAUGE
18 sts and 25 rows = 4" (10 cm) in Garter stitch (knit every row)

Afghan

Using A, CO 135 sts; begin Garter st (knit every row).
Stripe Sequence: * Knit 8 rows A, 4 rows B, 7 rows A, 3 rows C, 1 row B; repeat from * until piece measures approximately 56½", ending after finishing 1 row of B, thus completing the last repeat of Stripe sequence.
Knit 7 rows A, 4 rows B, and 8 rows A.
BO all sts.

Finishing
Using A, cut yarn into 12" lengths.
Fringe: Using 4 strands for each Fringe, beginning at CO edge at corner of Afghan, work Fringe in approximately 1" intervals along edge (see Special Techniques, page 175). Repeat for BO edge.
* Beginning at one corner, separate each Fringe in half, and regroup with half the strands from the next Fringe. Using a separate strand of yarn, tie newly-formed Fringe together approx 1" from edge of throw; continue along entire row of Fringe at both ends of Afghan. Repeat from * once more.

JOLENE TREACE

Keefely Mittens

For JoLene Treace, Christmas conjures up memories of her Norwegian grandmother and the wonderful cookies she made. Called keefelys, they were crescent-shaped, with a thin, pastrylike outer layer, a filling of ground walnuts inside, and a sprinkling of powdered sugar on top (see recipe on page 101). JoLene designed these mittens in honor of her grandmother and those unforgettable cookies. In addition to the stranded patterning common to Norwegian knitwear designs, these mittens fittingly incorporate a Turkish stitch pattern known as "walnut meats" in the cuff.

FINISHED MEASUREMENTS
8" in circumference by 11¼" long

YARN
Goddess Yarns Julia (50% lambswool / 25% kid mohair / 25% alpaca; 93 yards / 50 grams): 2 skeins (MC), 2 skeins (A), and 1 skein (B) Mittens shown in #4936 blue thyme, #6936 deep blue sea, and #3961 lady's mantle

NEEDLES
One set of five double-pointed needles (dpn) size US 5 (3.75 mm) OR
Two circular (circ) needles size US 5 (3.75 mm) Change needle size if necessary to obtain correct gauge.

NOTIONS
Stitch markers, waste yarn, yarn needle

GAUGE
30 sts and 30 rows = 4" (10 cm) in Color pattern from Chart

NOTES
* If using two circular needles, both are working needles. Use one circular needle to work each side of the mitten.
* Rows 33–49 are the Thumb Gusset shaping rows; the chart for the Thumb Gusset also has rows numbered 33–49, and Mitten Chart indicates where these rows should be worked. The remaining Thumb rows, Rows 50–64, are worked when the Thumb is worked.

Mittens

Cuff
Using Double Start CO (see Special Techniques, page 174) and A, CO 60 sts. Divide sts evenly on working needles. Join for working in the rnd, being careful not to twist sts; place marker (pm) for beginning of rnd.
Change to St st and begin Chart, Rnd 1. Work Rnds 1–31, changing colors as indicated.
Rnd 32: Work 28 sts, pm, work 3 sts, pm, work to end of rnd.

Thumb Gusset
Rnd 33: Work increases as indicated on first and third sts between the markers placed on Rnd 32; and AT THE SAME TIME, begin Thumb Gusset Chart on center st.
When increases are complete there will be 9 sts on either side of center st, for a total of 19 sts in the Thumb Gusset—21 sts between the markers.

Mitten Body
Rnd 50: Work to marker, k1, CO 1 st using Backward Loop CO (see Special Techniques, page 174); place 19 Thumb Gusset sts on waste yarn; work to end of rnd. Continue from Chart through Rnd 71.

Mitten Top
Rnds 72–84: Work decreases as indicated on Chart—8 sts remain.
Break yarn, leaving a 6" tail; thread tail through remaining sts, pull tight to close top of Mitten, and secure to WS. Weave in ends.

Thumb

Place Thumb Gusset sts onto working needles.

Rnd 50—Thumb Gusset Chart: Work 19 sts from Chart; pick up and knit 7 sts across top of thumb opening as follows:

Pick up and knit 3 sts evenly spaced between the gusset sts and the CO st; pick up 1 st from the CO st; pick up and knit 3 sts evenly spaced up to the gusset sts.

Rnd 51: Work double decreases as shown on Chart to decrease the 7 picked up sts to 3 sts.

Rnds 52–60: Continue following Chart.

Rnd 61–64: Shape Thumb by working decreases as indicated on Chart—6 sts remain. Break yarn leaving a 4" tail. Complete as for Mitten Top.

Finishing

Wash and block.

THUMB GUSSET CHART

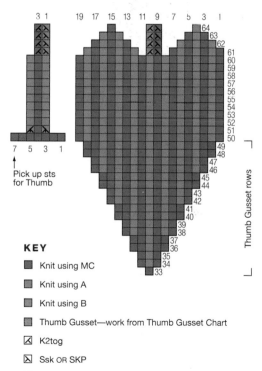

Pick up sts for Thumb

Thumb Gusset rows

KEY

■ Knit using MC

■ Knit using A

■ Knit using B

■ Thumb Gusset—work from Thumb Gusset Chart

◿ K2tog

◻ Ssk OR SKP

ꞁ Lifted increase—right: Knit into st below next st on left-hand needle, then knit stitch on left-hand needle.

˥ Lifted increase—left: Knit next stitch on left-hand needle; with the left-hand needle, pick up loop from stitch below stitch just worked, knit the picked up loop.

U Cast-on

◻ Sk2p: Slip 1, k2tog, PSSO

◿ K3tog

keefely mittens

GRANDMA ELAINE'S KEEFELY COOKIES

The recipe for these rich nut cookies comes from designer JoLene Treace's grandmother, Elaine Christine Rhodes, who was born in Wisconsin to Norwegian immigrants in 1917. Their crescent shape and powdered sugar coating give them a distinctive holiday look. They are a sure crowd pleaser but are labor intensive to make because you need to roll out the dough and add the walnut filling for each cookie individually. If you have time to give your holiday cookies this kind of tender loving care, this recipe is an excellent choice. If you're in a hurry, pull a quicker recipe from your files.

Dough

8 ounces (2 sticks) unsalted butter, softened

5 large egg yolks (reserve half of the whites for the filling)

½ cup sour cream

Zest and juice of ½ large lemon (zest is yellow part of skin; do not use bitter white pith)

3 cups all-purpose flour

Filling

About 2½ large egg whites (reserved when making dough)

½ pound powdered sugar, plus extra for dusting cookies after baking

Juice of ½ large lemon (reserved when making dough)

1 pound walnuts, finely ground

Make Dough

In a large bowl, using an electric mixer set at medium speed, cream the butter. Beat in the egg yolks, sour cream, lemon zest, and flour, and beat just until the dough is smooth and holds together; do not overbeat. Form the dough into individual balls about the size of a walnut (approximately 1 tablespooon dough per ball), place the balls into several gallon-size zip-shut bags (about 10–20 balls per bag), and refrigerate overnight.

Make Filling

In a medium-sized bowl, combine all of the filling ingredients. Divide between 2 bowls, cover, and refrigerate for about 30 minutes or until needed.

Assemble and Bake Cookies

Preheat the oven to 375°F. Set aside an ungreased cookie sheet.

On an open counter space, prepare 2 sheets parchment paper between which you can roll the balls of dough (alternatively, cut open the sides of a one-gallon zip-shut bag and roll the dough between the 2 layers). Remove 1 bag of balls and 1 bowl of filling from the refrigerator. One at a time, roll out each ball thinly into a rectangle or oval about 6" long. Place 1–2 teaspoons filling down the center of the oval so it forms a line about 4½–5" long. Seal the long seam of the oval so the filling is enclosed, pinch the ends shut, and roll into a thin rope (no larger than ½" in diameter). Bend the rope slightly to create a crescent shape and place on the cookie sheet. The dough and filling are very sticky; if necessary, lightly dust your hands with flour while you're working and/or return the dough and filling to the refrigerator to chill.

Bake the cookies for 10–13 minutes, until they are a little brown on the bottom. Transfer the cookies to a wire rack to cool for a few minutes, then arrange in a single layer on a plate and sift powdered sugar over them. (Alternatively, pour a generous amount of the sugar into a cake pan and dredge the cookies in it.)

Makes about 40 cookies.

KIM HAMLIN *Flap-Top Mittens*

It's said that mittens keep hands warmer than gloves—there's more space inside a mitten to trap air, and your fingers can share body heat in a way they can't when they're isolated in gloves. Still, Kim Hamlin notes, nothing is colder than having to remove your whole mitten to do a task. Her flap-top mitten is the perfect solution. Flap up, your fingers are kept cozy by thick wool and your own body heat. Flap down, they're free to tie skate laces or press cell phone buttons while the rest of your hand stays warm.

FINISHED MEASUREMENTS
To fit Child (Woman, Man)
7 (8¾, 10½)" in circumference
by 7 (10½, 12½)" long

YARN
Alchemy Lone Star (55% mohair /
45% merino wool; 135 yards / 100 grams):
1 skein each MC and CC for all sizes
Shown in the following colors:
#43e canopy (MC) and #65e dragon (CC)
for child's mittens (see page 104);
#31e olive branch (MC) and #41a vermillion (CC)
for woman's mittens (see left)

NEEDLES
One set of five double-pointed needles
(dpn) size US 5 (3.75 mm)
One set of five double-pointed needles
size US 7 (4.5 mm)
Change needle size if necessary to obtain
correct gauge.

NOTIONS
Yarn needle, stitch markers, waste yarn,
two double-ended stitch holders

GAUGE
18 sts and 24 rows = 4" (10 cm) in Stockinette
stitch (St st) using larger needles

Right Mitten

Using smaller needles and CC, CO 30 (38, 46) sts. Join for working in the rnd, being careful not to twist sts; place marker (pm) for beginning of rnd. Begin k1, p1 rib; work even until piece measures 1 (2¼, 2¾)" from the beginning.

Change to larger needles, MC and St st; * k15 (19, 23), M1; repeat from * around—32 (40, 48) sts. Work even as established until piece measures 2 (3½, 4¼)" from the beginning.

Thumb Gusset
Rnd 1: K15 (19, 23), pm, M1, k2, M1, pm, knit to end—34 (42, 50) sts.
Rnd 2 and all even numbered rnds: Knit.
Rnd 3: Knit to marker, slip marker (sm), M1, knit to next marker, M1, sm, knit to end—36 (42, 44) sts.
Repeat Rnds 2 and 3 until there are 10 (12, 14) sts between markers.
Next Rnd: Knit to 1 st before marker, M1, k1, transfer stitches between markers onto waste yarn, k1, M1, knit to end—32 (40, 48) sts. Continue even in St st until piece measures 4 (5, 6)" from the beginning.

Prepare Flap
[K1, wrapping yarn twice around needle] 18 (22, 26) times; knit across to last 2 sts, repeat [ ] twice.
Note: It will look like you have a lot more sts on your needles now. For next rnd, using more than one spare dpn to hold slipped sts makes it easier.
Next Rnd: [Knit next st, slip second loop onto a smaller dpn at front of work] 18 (22, 26) times; knit across to last 2 sts, repeat [ ] twice. Transfer slipped sts [loops] on spare dpn to st holders or waste yarn. Knit 2 rnds.

Change to smaller needles.

ALL SIZES
Next Rnd: Skp, k12 (16, 20), k2tog, skp, knit to last 2 sts, k2tog—28 (36, 44) sts remain.

Next Rnd: Skp, k14 (18), k2tog, skp, knit to last
2 sts, k2tog—32 (40) sts remain.

ALL SIZES

Work even as established until piece measures
5½ (7, 8½)" from beginning; BO all sts.

Flap

Transfer sts from holders onto smaller dpn
as follows:
With Mitten palm side up, place the 2 far right
sts and 2 far left sts on Needle 1 [there will be
a large gap between sts across the palm];
place 8 (10, 12) sts each on Needles 2 and 3.

Using CC, k2 from Needle 1, CO 12 (16, 20) sts
across gap, k2; knit across Needles 2 and 3—
32 (40, 48) sts total.
*Note: If desired, the sts on Needle 1 may be
divided onto 2 needles.*

Change to k1, p1 rib; work even for 1".

Change to larger needles, MC and St st;
work even until piece measures 1½ (2, 2½)"
above ribbing.

Begin decreasing as follows:
Rnd 1: K16 (20, 24), pm, knit to end.
Rnd 2: [Skp, knit to 2 sts before marker,
k2tog] twice.
Rnd 3: Knit.

CHILD SIZE ONLY

Repeat Rnds 2 and 3 four more times—
12 sts remain.

ADULT SIZES ONLY

Rnd 4: Knit.
Repeat Rnds 2–4 once more.
Repeat Rnds 2 and 3 five (seven) more times—
12 (12) sts remain.

Break yarn leaving a 4" tail and thread through
remaining sts. Draw tight to close and fasten off;
secure on WS. Weave in ends.

Thumb

Place sts from waste yarn onto larger dpn. Pick
up and knit 4 sts around top of Thumb opening.
Join for working in the rnd; in St st, work even
until Thumb measures 2½ (3¼, 4)" from beginning of gusset.
Decrease Rnd: * K2tog; repeat from * around.
Break yarn leaving a 4" tail and thread through
remaining sts. Draw tight to close and fasten off;
secure on WS. Weave in ends.

Left Mitten

Work as for Right Mitten until Prepare Flap.
Change double-wrapped sts to first 2 and
last 18 (22, 26) sts.

Continue with the rest of the instructions as
written for Right Mitten.

DRESSING UP

Sweaters, Shawls, and Party Hats

Wrap yourself up like a present with these glorious little scarves, crafted to look like curled holiday ribbon. Wear them coiled around your neck for a ruff look, or toss one end over a shoulder for a boa effect. Better yet, tie them around a wrapped present for an exquisite package wrapping that doubles as a spontaneous gift.

FINISHED MEASUREMENTS
Version 1 (see left): 38" long by 4" wide
Version 2 (see right): 22" long by 4" wide

YARN
Version 1
Classic Elite Lush (50% angora / 50% wool; 123 yards / 50 grams): 4 skeins #4441 dark red (MC)
Rowan Lurex Shimmer (80% viscose / 20% polyester; 105 yards / 25 grams): 4 skeins #331 claret (CC)
Version 2
Rowan Kid Silk Haze (70% super kid mohair / 30% silk; 230 yards / 25 grams): 3 skeins #597 jelly (MC)

NEEDLES
Two 32" circular (circ) needles size US 8 (5 mm)
Change needle size if necessary to obtain correct gauge.
Note: When it becomes hard to work on one needle alone due to the large number of stitches, add the second needle, place stoppers on ends, and work back and forth.

NOTIONS
Yarn needle, 2 needle stoppers

GAUGE
16 sts and 24 rows = 4" (10 cm) in Stockinette stitch (St st)

Scarf

Using MC, CO 100 (70) sts.
Row 1: Purl
Row 2: K1-f/b in each st across, doubling the number of sts on the needle—200 (140) sts.
Rows 3–5: Change to St st; work even for 3 rows.
Row 6: Repeat Row 2—400 (280) sts.
Rows 7–9: Work even in St st.
Row 10: Repeat Row 2—800 (560) sts.
Rows 11–15: Work even in St st.
Row 16: Repeat Row 2—1600 (1120) sts.
Rows 17–19: Repeat Rows 7–9.

VERSION 1 ONLY
Change to a double strand of CC.
Row 20: Repeat Row 2—3200 sts.

BOTH VERSIONS
BO all sts loosely.

Finishing
Weave in ends.
Steam edge of Version 1 to prevent curling.

Sparkly Kiss Cap

This lighthearted baby hat ensures that everyone in your family can get into the spirit of the season—no matter how little they are. A slip of French ribbon—the kind that's edged with fine wire to hold its shape—tops off the hat with a tag, replicating the famous chocolate confection it mimics to the smallest detail.

SIZES

Child's Newborn (Infant, Small, Medium)
To fit 0–6 months (6–12 months, 12–18 months, 24+ months)
Shown in size 12–18 months

FINISHED MEASUREMENTS

17½ (18, 19¾, 21½)" circumference

YARN

Filatura di Crosa No Smoking (66% viscose / 34% polyester; 82 yards / 25 grams): 2 (3, 4, 4) balls #101 (use double strand throughout)

NEEDLES

One 16" circular (circ) needle size US 7 (4.5 mm)
One set of five double-pointed needles (dpn) size US 7 (4.5 mm)
Change needle size if necessary to obtain correct gauge.

NOTIONS

Stitch marker, knitting elastic, 1½–2" wide white or transparent wired ribbon (wider for larger sizes), yarn needle, sewing needle and thread; Fray Check

GAUGE

20 sts and 22 rows = 4" (10 cm) in Stockinette stitch (St st) using 2 strands yarn held together

Cap

Using circ needle, knitting elastic, and a doubled strand of yarn, CO 82 (84, 90, 96) sts. Join for working in the rnd, being careful not to twist sts; place marker (pm) for beginning of rnd. Begin k2, p2 rib; work even for 4 (4, 6, 6) rnds. Break off knitting elastic.

Change to St st; increase 6 (6, 9, 12) sts evenly around on next rnd—88 (90, 99, 108) sts. Work even as established until piece measures 4 (4½, 5, 5½)" from the beginning.

Shape Top

Note: Begin with Rnd 3 for Newborn size. Change to dpn when necessary for number of sts remaining.

Rnd 1: * K7, k2tog-tbl; repeat from * around—88 (80, 88, 96) sts remain.
Rnd 2: Knit.
Rnd 3: * K6, k2tog-tbl; repeat from * around—77 (70, 77, 84) sts remain.
Rnd 4: Knit.
Rnd 5: * K5, k2tog-tbl; repeat from * around—66 (60, 66, 72) sts remain.
Rnd 6: Knit.
Rnd 7: * K4, k2tog-tbl; repeat from * around—55 (50, 55, 60) sts remain.
Rnds 8–11: Knit.
Rnd 12: * K3, k2tog-tbl; repeat from * around—44 (40, 44, 48) sts remain.
Rnds 13 and 14: Knit.
Rnd 15: * K2, k2tog-tbl; repeat from * around—33 (30, 33, 36) sts remain.
Rnds 16 and 17: Knit.
Rnd 18: * K1, k2tog-tbl; repeat from * around—22 (20, 22, 24) sts remain.
** Work 2 (2, 3, 3) rnds even in St st.
Next Rnd: *K2tog-tbl; repeat from * around—11 (10, 11, 12) sts remain. Repeat from ** once, ending second decrease rnd k1 (0, 1, 0)—6 (5, 6, 6) sts remain. Thread yarn through remaining sts and fasten off; secure on WS. Weave in ends and block lightly if needed.

Finishing

Cut a piece of ribbon 6–12" in length; play with length and different ways wire bends to get desired look. Cut ribbon on diagonal (this will be end that sticks out of Hat) and apply Fray Check to seal. Thread ribbon through top of Hat and stitch in place with needle and thread.

Who says that Santa is just for kids? Don this cap and show the world that the jolly old elf isn't only a children's fiction. Knit with bulky, luxurious alpaca yarn, complete with a "fur" trim of fat bobbles, this is a fast, fun project suitable for revelers of any age.

SIZES
X-Small (Small, Medium, Large)
To fit Infant (Child, Woman, Man)
Shown in size Medium

FINISHED MEASUREMENTS
18 (20, 22, 24)" circumference, excluding Bobble Band

YARN
Blue Sky Worsted Hand Dyes (50% alpaca / 50% wool; 100 yards / 100 grams): 1 hank #2000 red (MC)
Blue Sky Bulky (50% alpaca / 50% wool; 45 yards / 100 grams): 2 hanks #1004 polar bear (CC)

NEEDLES
One 16" circular (circ) needle size US 9 (5.5 mm)
One set of five double-pointed needles (dpn) size US 9 (5.5 mm)
One 16" circular (circ) needle size US 11 (8 mm) for Bobble Band
Change needle size if necessary to obtain correct gauge.

NOTIONS
Stitch markers, yarn needle

GAUGE
16 sts and 24 rows = 4" (10 cm) in Stockinette stitch (St st) using smaller needles and Blue Sky Worsted

NOTES
✴ This hat is worked in St st in-the-round from lower edge to Crown. Stitches are picked up around CO edge to work Bobble Band.

✴ **Make Bobble (mb):** [Yo, k1] 3 times in next st to increase to 6 sts, turn; slip 1, p5, turn; slip 1, k5, turn; [p2tog] 3 times, turn; sk2p—1 st remains.

Hat

Crown
Note: Change to dpn when necessary for number of sts remaining.
Using smaller circ needle and MC, CO 72 (81, 90, 99) sts loosely. Join for working in the rnd, being careful not to twist sts; place marker (pm) for beginning of rnd.
Rnd 1: [K24 (27, 30, 33), pm] twice, knit to end—72 (81, 90, 99) sts.
Rnd 2: Knit.
Rnd 3: * Ssk, knit to next marker; repeat from * around—69 (78, 87, 96) sts remain.
Rnd 4: Knit.
Repeat Rnds 3 and 4—11 (12, 13, 16) more times—36 (42, 48, 48) sts remain.
Repeat Rnd 3–8 (10, 12, 12) more times—12 sts remain.
Next Rnd: * K1, ssk; repeat from * around—8 sts remain.
Last Rnd: * K2tog; repeat from * around—4 sts remain.
Break yarn. With tail and yarn needle, thread end through remaining sts and tug gently to tighten; fasten off. Secure to WS.

Bobble Band
With RS facing, using smaller needles and MC, pick up 38 (42, 46, 50) sts evenly around CO edge. Change to circ needle and CC.
Rnd 1 (RS): Knit; join for working in the rnd; pm for beginning of rnd.
Rnd 2: Knit.
Rnd 3: * K1, mb; repeat from * around.
Rnd 4: Knit.
Bind off all sts loosely.

Pompom
Make one 3" Pompom (see Special Techniques, page 176). Sew Pompom to top of Hat using ends of tie. Weave in ends.

CARRIE BRENNER
Zigzag Poncho/Skirt and Dog Sweater

This versatile piece had its beginnings as a poncho (see page 114)—until the model wearing it pulled it down over her hips. At that moment, it was transformed into a playful skirt (see right). When worn as a poncho, the ribbed neck can be left flat or folded over—even pulled down over the shoulders. The easy-to-master zigzag pattern—a more feminine take on stripes—works up quickly and creates a self-scalloping edge. For fun, knit a complementary sweater for Fido.

FINISHED MEASUREMENTS
Poncho/Skirt: Neck circumference 24"; length 24"; lower edge circumference 72"
Dog Sweater: Neck circumference 10"; length 12½"; body circumference 21"

YARN
Alchemy Lone Star (55% mohair / 45% merino wool; 135 yards / 100 grams)
Poncho/Skirt: 3 skeins #64f Scarlett's dark secret (burgundy; A); 2 skeins each #41a vermillion (pink; B), #87e Mississippi mud (purple; C), #65e dragon (chartreuse; D), #43e canopy (mossy green; E), and #37e twig (mauve; F)
Dog Sweater: 1 skein each A, B, C, D, E and F

NEEDLES
Poncho/Skirt: One each 24" and 32" circular needle size US 8 (5 mm)
Dog Sweater: One each 12" and 16" circular (circ) needle size US 8 (5 mm)
Optional: One set of five double-pointed needles (dpn) size US 8 (5 mm), instead of 12" circ needle
Change needle size if necessary to obtain correct gauge.

NOTIONS
Stitch marker, yarn needle

GAUGE
15 sts and 20 rows = 3" (7.6 cm) in Zigzag pattern

NOTES
✢ **Ribbing Pattern:**
Poncho/Skirt and Dog Sweater
K1, p1 rib [k3, p3 rib] (multiple of 2 [6] sts; 1-rnd repeat)
All rnds: * K1 (3), p1 (3); repeat from * around.

✢ **Zigzag Pattern:** Poncho/Skirt
(multiple of 15 sts; 14-rnd repeat)
Note: Move markers up each rnd until pattern becomes established; continue using them throughout if desired.
Rnd 1: * [K1, yo, k1] in next st, place marker (pm) before center increase st, k5, sk2p, pm on center decrease st, k6; repeat from * around.
Rnd 2 and all even rnds: Knit.
Rnd 3: * Knit to marked increase st, [k1, yo, k1] in next st; repeat from * around.
Rnd 5: * Knit to marked increase st, [k1, yo, k1] in next st, knit to 1 st before marked decrease st, sk2p; repeat from * around.
Rnds 7, 9, and 11: Repeat Rnd 5.
Rnd 13: Repeat Rnd 3.
Rnd 14: Knit.
Repeat Rnds 1–14 for Zigzag pattern in Stripe Sequence.

✢ **Zigzag Pattern:** Dog Sweater
Work Rnds 1 and 2 of Zigzag pattern for Poncho/Skirt in Stripe Sequence.
Repeat these 2 rnds throughout.

✢ **Stripe Sequence**
In Zigzag pattern, * work 6 rnds B, 4 rnds C, 6 rnds D, 4 rnds E, 6 rnds F, 4 rnds B, 6 rnds C, 4 rnds D, 6 rnds E, 4 rnds A.
For Poncho/Skirt, repeat from * once; for Dog Sweater, work Stripe sequence once, then work 6 rnds B.

✢ Use Jogless Color Change (see Special Techniques, page 175) to minimize disruption of the color patterns.

Poncho/Skirt

Collar

Beginning at neck edge, using A and 24" circ needle, CO 138 sts. Join for working in the rnd, being careful not to twist sts; place marker (pm) for beginning of rnd. Begin k3, p3 rib.
Work even for 50 rnds.
Knit one rnd, decreasing 3 sts evenly around—135 sts remain.

Body

Begin Zigzag pattern in Stripe Sequence as given on page 112; change to longer needle when sufficient sts have been increased.
Work Stripe sequence twice—piece measures approximately 22" long, excluding neck ribbing.
Note: For longer Poncho/Skirt, continue as established until piece measures 2" shorter than desired length.
Lower Edging: Change to A; work in k1, p1 rib for 2", continuing increases and decreases as established.
BO all sts in rib.

Dog Sweater

NOTES

Sizing Dog Sweater

✤ This Dog Sweater is essentially a tube with front leg openings. The body can easily be sized up or down in 3" increments (one pattern repeat) by adding or subtracting repeats over the Back and/or the Under-Section.

Example: This sweater is 6" between the front legs and 15" over the Back; a smaller size could be 3" between the front legs and 12" over the Back.

✤ Measure around the dog's neck (not too tightly) and multiply by the gauge to get your CO number of sts, then adjust this figure to fit into the multiple of the ribbing, which is 6.

✤ Work in k3, p3 rib for desired length, then increase evenly around to the number of sts needed for the Body (be sure the number is a multiple of 15).

✤ Work even to the top of the front legs; work the Leg Openings to desired length; join and continue even to desired length, less 2" (don't forget to take gender into account); then work 2" in rib at lower edge, and leg ribbing.

Beginning at neck edge, using A and 12" circ needle (or dpn), CO 54 sts. Join for working in the round, being careful not to twist sts; place marker (pm) for beginning of rnd. Begin k3, p3 rib.

Work even for 20 rnds.

Change to 16" circ needle; knit 1 rnd, increasing 51 sts evenly around—105 sts.

Body

Begin Zigzag pattern in Stripe Sequence as given on page 112.

Work even until piece measures 2" from the beginning, ending with Rnd 1.

Leg Openings

Under-Section: K7, turn; p30, turn; leave remaining 75 sts on holder for Back.

Working on these 30 sts only, continue as follows:

Row 1 (RS): K1, k2tog, k5, [k1, yo, k1] in next st, k5, sk2p, k6, [k1, yo, k1] in next st, k3, ssk, k1.

Row 2: Purl.

Repeat Rows 1 and 2 in Stripe Sequence for approximately 2", ending with Row 1.

Back

With WS facing, continuing in Stripe Sequence, join yarn to remaining sts, p75, turn.

Row 1 (RS): K1, k2tog, k5, * [k1, yo, k1] in next st, k5, sk2p, k6; repeat from * to last 7 sts, end [k1, yo, k1] in next st, k3, ssk, k1.

Row 2: Purl.

Repeat Rows 1 and 2 in Stripe Sequence until Back measures same as Under-Section, ending with Row 1.

Joining Rnd

Knit across 30 Under-section sts, then knit across 75 Back sts—105 sts. Join for working in the round; continue in Stripe Sequence as for Body until piece measures 12" from the beginning, excluding neck ribbing, or to 2" less than desired length, decreasing one st on last row. Change to A; work in k1, p1 rib for 2". BO in rib.

Leg Ribbing

Using dpn, pick up and knit 20 sts around Leg Opening. Work even in k1, p1 rib for 2"; BO in rib.

Crisscross Shrug

Part shawl, part sweater, part shrug—this unique accessory by visionary designer Norah Gaughan combines and reinterprets all three. It is worked in two separate pieces and two harmonic colors; each sleeve loops around the opposite shoulder. Worn singly or together, they're a unique—and warm—way to top off a camisole, a sleeveless cocktail dress, or even a denim jacket.

FINISHED MEASUREMENTS
Length cuff to shoulder: 34"
Width at widest point: 14"

YARN
GGH Aspen (50% merino wool / 50% acrylic;
57 meters / 50 grams): 5 balls each
#26 (dark green) and #27 (light green)

NEEDLES
One pair straight needles size US 10.5 (6.5 mm)
One pair straight needles size US 13 (9 mm)
Change needle size if necessary to obtain correct gauge.

NOTIONS
1 yard round elastic, yarn needle

GAUGE
10 sts and 14 rows = 4" (10 cm) in Stockinette stitch (St st) using larger needles

Shrug

Using one of the two yarn colors and larger needles, CO 18 sts.

Establish Pattern
Row 1 (RS): Slip 2 sts as if to purl, p1, k2, place marker (pm), knit across to last 3 sts, p1, k2.
Row 2: Slip 2 sts as if to purl, k1, purl across to last 3 sts, k1, p2.
Repeat Rows 1 and 2 three times—
8 rows completed.
Row 9 (Increase Row): Work to marker, M1, slip marker (sm), k8, M1, work to end—20 sts.
Repeat Rows 2–9 eight times—36 sts.
Repeat Rows 2–8 once more.
Shape Shoulder (Short rows): * (RS) Work 33 sts, turn (leave last 3 sts of row unworked). (WS) Yo, work to end of row.
Next Row (RS): Work 33 sts, p2tog [the yo and the next st], work to end. Work 5 rows even.
Repeat from * 6 more times. Work 2 rows even.

Decrease Row (RS): Work to 2 sts before marker, ssk, sm, k8, k2tog, work to end—
34 sts remain.
Repeat Decrease row every 8 rows 8 times—
18 sts remain.
Work even for 7 rows, ending with a WS row.

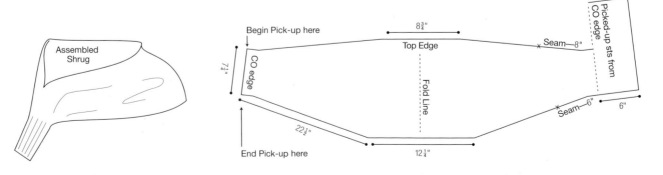

Cuff

(RS) Change to smaller needles; k2, k2tog, knit across to last 4 sts, k2tog, k2—16 sts remain; DO NOT TURN.

Fold shawl in half, with WS's facing each other; continuing with working yarn, with RS of CO edge facing, pick up and knit 14 sts across CO edge, taking care that shawl is not twisted—30 sts.

(WS) Change to k2, p2 rib, beginning and ending p2. Work even for 6"; BO all sts in rib.

Finishing

Block pieces lightly with steam. Sew cuff seam, and continue seam for 6" past cuff. Sew opposite seam (top edge) together for 8" past cuff.

Tie elastic just inside top edge, at end of seam, leaving a 2" tail. Thread yarn needle with elastic and weave through casing created by slipped sts. Adjust both ends of elastic to fit the wearer and fasten securely. Weave in ends.

Knit a second shrug in remaining color of yarn.

CINDY TAYLOR *Santa Lucia Crown*

In Swedish tradition, there exists a beloved saint named Santa Lucia. Originally a young Sicilian woman, Lucia was imprisoned at her husband's bidding—and ultimately killed—for giving her wedding gifts to the poor. Centuries later, in the midst of a famine in Sweden, she miraculously appeared with food and drink, and so she is honored today as one who brings light and warmth and sustenance to those who need it most. When Lucia appears—as she frequently does on the morning of December 13 in Swedish homes—she's dressed in white, wearing on her head a wreath ablaze with candles. While we can't endorse wearing lit candles on your head, we do invite you to try this crown, a lively creation that could easily double as an Advent wreath or centerpiece. It's a funky wreath, knitted with leaves and loops of tweedy greens and golds, attached on an I-cord base that keeps its shape with florist's wire. It takes a revolutionary spirit to wear this wreath to the office holiday party—but then, that's Lucia.

FINISHED MEASUREMENTS
Approximately 22" around, excluding ties

YARN
Rowan Biggy Print (100% wool; 32 yards / 100 grams): 2 balls #245 troll
Rowan Yorkshire Tweed DK (100% wool; 123 yards / 50 grams): 1 ball each #348 lime leaf and #349 frog
Rowan Yorkshire Tweed Chunky (100% wool; 109 yards / 100 grams): 1 ball #557 olive oil
Rowanspun Aran (100% wool; 217 yards / 100 grams): 1 ball #972 hardy
Rowan Cork (95% extra-fine merino / 5% nylon; 120 yards / 50 grams): 1 ball #039 gleam
Rowan Summer Tweed (70% silk / 30% cotton; 117 yards / 50 grams): 1 ball each #504 gold and #514 reed

NEEDLES
One pair straight needles size US 9 (5.5 mm)
One pair straight needles size US 15 (10 mm)
Change needle size if necessary to obtain correct gauge.

NOTIONS
Crochet hook size I/9 (6.5 mm)
Crochet hook size N/15 (10 mm)
Yarn needle, florist's wire

GAUGE
Not critical for this project

KNITTING FOR OTHERS

*If you wish to extend your holiday giving to people in need
but are not sure how to begin, consider knitting for the following organizations. For a more extensive list of charitable knitting
opportunities, visit www.interweave.com/knit/charities.asp.
For listings of charity knitting organized by state, visit
www.woolworks.org/charity.html.*

Warm Up America! Foundation

Attention: WSD, 2500 Lowell Rd., Ranlo, NC 28054;
(800) 662-9999; www.warmupamerica.com
Whether you contribute one 7" by 9" knitted square or
an entire afghan, you can help warm and comfort people
in homeless shelters, battered women's shelters, AIDS
facilities, hospitals, hospices, and children's homes.

Afghans for Afghans

c/o AFSC Collection Center, 65 9th Street,
San Francisco, CA 94103; www.afghansforafghans.org
Hats, mittens, sweaters, vests, and of course, afghans—
all are warm, welcome necessities for people in war-
ravaged Afghanistan.

Project Linus

P.O. Box 5621, Bloomington, IL 61702-5621;
(309) 664-7814; www.projectlinus.org
Hand-knitted blankets provide "security" to children
in need around the world, whether seriously ill,
traumatized, or, as the website puts it, otherwise
"in need of a big hug."

Binky Patrol

P.O. Box 1468, Laguna Beach, CA 92652-1468;
(949) 916-5926; www.binkypatrol.org
Through this organization, handmade, soft, washable
blankets are given to children and teens in need across
the country.

Crown

Petals
Make 18 (3 each in gleam, gold, reed, lime leaf,
olive oil, and hardy).
CO 2 sts.
Row 1: K1, yo, k1–3 sts.
Row 2: [K1, yo] 2 times, k1–5 sts.
Row 3: K2, yo, k1, yo, k2–7 sts.
Row 4: K3, yo, k1, yo, k3–9 sts.
Row 4: Knit.
Row 5: K1, k2tog, k3, k2tog, k1–7 sts.
BO all sts.

Loft Leaf
Make 6 (3 each in olive oil and lime leaf).
CO 3 sts.
Row 1: Knit.
Row 2: Knit.
Row 3: [K1, yo] 2 times, k1—5 sts.
Rows 4–11: Knit.
Row 12: K2tog, k1, k2tog—3 sts.
Rows 13 and 14: Knit 2 rows.
Row 15: Sk2p—1 st remains; fasten off.

Floop
Make 9 (3 in lime leaf, 6 in hardy).
CO 3 sts.
Knit 24 rows.
BO all sts.

Sprout
Make 14 (3 each in olive oil and gleam,
4 each in lime leaf, gold, and frog).
CO 15 sts.
Knit 1 row.
BO all sts.

Loop

Make as many as desired in all colors to fill in Headband.

Using crochet hook and leaving 4" long tail, work crochet chains (see Special Techniques, page 174) of varying lengths; fasten off, leaving a tail for attaching chain to Headband.

Bud

Make as many as desired in all colors to fill in Headband.

Using crochet hook and leaving 4" long tail, work crochet chains of varying lengths; fasten off, leaving a tail. Work tail back through chain several sts from the end, creating a small bud.

Headband

Measure head for fit. Using larger needles and Biggy Print, CO 3 sts. Attach florist's wire and work I cord (see Special Techniques, page 175) with yarn, enclosing the wire within, until Headband is 2" shorter than your head measurement. Fasten off.

Using crochet hook, work two 13" crochet chains for ties; fasten off. Using tail, attach chains to ends of Headband. Weave in ends.

Assembly

Petals, leaves, and embellishments are attached to one side of Headband only, so that none come between the crown and your hair. Attach the largest leaves evenly across the Headband, then cluster smaller leaves next to each of the larger leaves. Fill in spaces with Sprouts, Floops, Loops, and Buds. Attach one end of the Floop to the Headband, twisting it one or more times if desired, before securing the other end to the Headband in the same place; do the same for the Sprouts and Loops. Attach one end of the Bud to the Headband. Weave in ends.
Tie around head to wear.

While some children believe in Santa, Faina Letoutchaia grew up with this piece of Russian folklore: On the night before Christmas, children are visited by Grandfather Frost, who is always accompanied by his granddaughter Snegurochka (which might be translated into English as Snow Girl—as legend goes, she is made of snow). Snegurochka, who is about sixteen years old, rides with her Grandfather Frost in his sled, helps him with all his Christmas duties, and makes certain that no child is left without a present. Still, Faina explains, Snegurochka is a teenage girl, and like any teenage girl, she loves to go to parties. For Snegurochka and others (of any age) like her, Faina designed this sparkling, dramatic hat.

FINISHED MEASUREMENTS
Approximately 20" in circumference

YARN
Berroco Softwist (41% wool / 59% rayon; 100 yards / 50 grams): 2 skeins #9478 alizarin (MC)

NEEDLES
One set of five double-pointed needles (dpn) size US 5 (3.75 mm)
One 16" circular (circ) needle size US 5 (3.75 mm)
Change needle size if necessary to obtain correct gauge.

NOTIONS
Stitch markers, yarn needle, 2–3 yards waste yarn, beading needle, sewing needle, matching thread

BEADS
135 Swarovski crystal (4mm; Siam AB)
86 Swarovski crystal (6mm; Siam AB)
54 glass seed beads (#11; silverlined red)
172 glass seed beads (#8; silverlined red)
(See Sources for Supplies, page 182)

GAUGE
24 sts = 4" (10 cm) in Stockinette st (St st)

NOTES
⊹ This hat is intended to be worn pulled low on the forehead, with the beaded fringe right above the eyebrows.
⊹ It requires an elastic band to be inserted for a good, close fit. The hat will look floppy when knitted, but will become snug as soon as elastic is inserted and hat is blocked.
⊹ Read Lace Chart from right to left; only odd-numbered rnds are charted (except for last rnd); knit even for all even-numbered rnds.
⊹ When there are too many sts to work comfortably on dpn, transfer sts to circ needle and place st markers between repeats.

Hat

Beginning at top of Hat, using waste yarn, CO 6 sts; begin I-cord (see Special Techniques, page 175). Work for 1"; break off waste yarn. Change to MC, leaving a 4" tail. Join for working in the rnd; place marker (pm) for beginning of rnd.
Set-up Rnd: Knit, dividing sts onto 3 dpn; begin Chart.

Establish Pattern: Beginning Rnd 1, work Chart repeat 3 times around, one repeat on each needle.
Work Rnds 1–46 of Chart once, then repeat Rnds 45 and 46 until hat measures 7–7½" from beginning.

Picot edge: Knit 3 rnds; work Rnd 45 from Chart (fold line); knit 3 rnds. Do not bind off; break yarn, leaving a 50" tail.

Finishing

Measure a length of elastic to fit snugly around head plus a ½" overlap. Sew overlapped ends together to form a ring. Fold lower edge of Hat to WS on fold line to create Picot edge. Place elastic inside folded edge and whipstitch live sts to last eyelet rnd using 50" tail.

Remove waste yarn from top of Hat; thread 4" tail through 6 sts of the Set-up Rnd, pull tight to close top of Hat, and fasten off. Weave in ends.

Block Hat by placing on an inverted bowl approximately 20" in circumference. Spray generously with water to dampen and let dry completely.

Twisted Cord Fringe

Cut 32 pieces of yarn, each approximately 42" long. Make 32 Twisted Cords (see Special Techniques, page 178).

Place knotted end of Fringe at inside of picot edge so 7½" hangs freely. Using sewing thread, sew neatly and securely to the WS of Picot edge approximately ½" from lower edge. Remove overhand knots and cut excess neatly. Work a Fringe in each picot around Back of Hat.

LACE CHART

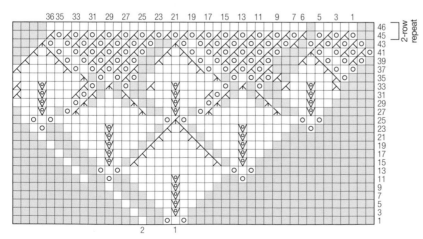

KEY

Note: Knit all even numbered rnds; they are not shown on chart, except for Rnd 46.

☐ Knit

⊡ Yo

▣ K1, yo, k1 all in same stitch

◩ K2tog

◪ Ssk

◩ Sk2p: Slip 1 knitwise, k2tog, pass slipped stitch over.

◪ Sskp: Ssk, return stitch to left-hand needle, pass the next stitch over the returned st, slip remaining st purlwise to right-hand needle.

☐ No stitch

Bead Embellishments

Using beading needle and sewing thread, sew a small (4mm) Swarovski crystal to the petals on the Hat, at each [k1, yo, k1] on the Chart.

Sew a Bead Fringe to each Picot across the Front of Hat; above each Twisted Cord Fringe across the Back; and to the end of each Fringe (see diagrams) as follows:

Bead Fringe

Using beading needle, attach thread to Picot point and string beads in this sequence: seed bead (#8), crystal (6mm), seed bead (#8), crystal (4mm), seed bead (#11). Then in opposite direction, skip seed bead (#11), insert needle into crystal (4mm), seed bead (#8), crystal (6mm), and seed bead (#8). When going back through the beads, take care not to split thread of the first pass.

Now all your beads are on the thread loop with the seed bead (#11) working as a stopper. Gently tighten this loop, so that all the beads are close to the Picot point, being careful not to pull too tightly. Secure thread invisibly behind Picot point. DO NOT BREAK THREAD, just go neatly to the next Picot point and attach the next group of beads.

Beaded Fringe (above cord Fringe): Work same as Bead Fringe above in this sequence: seed bead (#8), crystal (6mm), seed bead (#8). Then in opposite direction, skip seed bead (#8), insert needle into crystal (6mm) and seed bead (#8).

Beaded Fringe (ends of cord Fringe): Work same as Bead Fringe above, attaching each Bead Fringe to the end of each Twisted Cord Fringe. Secure invisibly and hide ends within Twisted Cord Fringe.

beading diagram

FRONT OF HAT

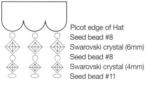

Picot edge of Hat
Seed bead #8
Swarovski crystal (6mm)
Seed bead #8
Swarovski crystal (4mm)
Seed bead #11

BACK OF HAT

○ Seed bead #8

◈ Swarovski crystal (6mm)

○ Seed bead #8

Yarn fringe

Sugarplum Pullover

This sweater was inspired by the exquisite Fair Isle knitwear made famous by the Swedish Bohus knitters, and a postcard depicting a wreath adorned with berries. It's made from a very soft wool and angora yarn—hand-dyed and thus subtly shaded—that is as lovely to knit with as it is to wear.

FINISHED MEASUREMENTS

Chest:
$35\frac{1}{2}$ (37, 40, $41\frac{1}{2}$, $44\frac{1}{4}$, $45\frac{3}{4}$, $48\frac{3}{4}$, 50, $52\frac{1}{4}$, $54\frac{1}{2}$)"
Pullover shown measures 37"

YARN

Kimmet Croft Fibers Softie (75% merino wool / 25% angora; 400 yards / 1 ounce): 8 (8, 10, 10, 11, 11, 12, 12, 14, 14) ounces #FF40 light brown (MC); 1 ounce each #FF132 dark green and #FF51 turquoise; $\frac{1}{2}$ ounce each #FF104 deep raspberry pink, #FF130 medium green, #FF116 light green; $\frac{1}{4}$ ounce each #FF102 fuchsia, #FF112 orange, #FF70 copper, #FF23 silver gray

NEEDLES

One 32" (80 cm) circular (circ) needle size US 3 (3.25 mm)
One 32" (80 cm) circular needle size US 5 (3.75 mm)
One 32" (80 cm) circular needle size US 7 (4.5 mm)
One set of five double-pointed needles (dpn) size US 3 (3.25 mm)
One set of five double-pointed needles size US 5 (3.75 mm)
Change needle size if necessary to obtain correct gauge.

NOTIONS

Stitch holders, stitch markers, yarn needle

GAUGE

22 sts and 34 rnds = 4" (10 cm) in Stockinette stitch (St st) using size US 7 needle
7 sts and 7 rnds = $\frac{3}{4}$" in Cross-Stitch rib using size US 5 needle

NOTES

⁜ **Cross-Stitch Rib** (multiple of 4 sts; 2-rnd repeat)
Rnd 1: * K2, p2; repeat from * around.
Rnd 2: * RT, p2; repeat from * around.
Repeat Rnds 1 and 2 for Cross-Stitch rib.

⁜ Use Jogless Color Change (see Special Techniques, page 175) to minimize disruption of the color pattern.

⁜ **RT**: K2tog, but do not drop sts from left-hand needle, insert right-hand needle between 2 sts just worked and **knit** the first stitch again, drop both sts from left-hand needle.

⁜ **RT-P**: K2tog, but do not drop sts from left-hand needle, insert right-hand needle between 2 sts just worked and **purl** the first stitch again, drop both sts from left-hand needle.

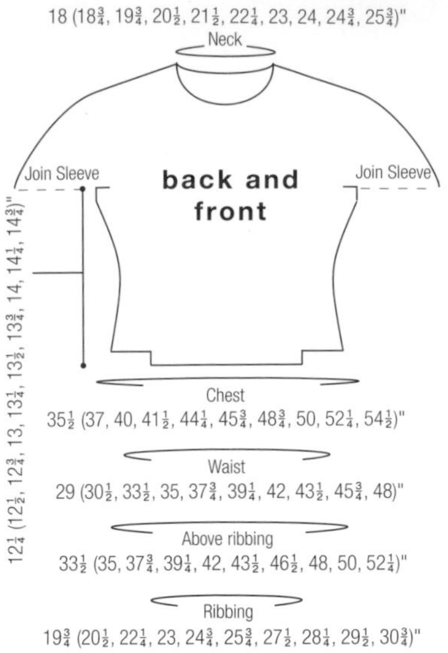

18 (18¾, 19¾, 20½, 21½, 22¼, 23, 24, 24¾, 25¾)"
Neck
Join Sleeve
back and front
Join Sleeve
12¼ (12½, 12¾, 13, 13¼, 13½, 13¾, 14, 14¼, 14¾)"
Chest
35½ (37, 40, 41½, 44¼, 45¾, 48¾, 50, 52¼, 54½)"
Waist
29 (30½, 33½, 35, 37¾, 39¼, 42, 43½, 45¾, 48)"
Above ribbing
33½ (35, 37¾, 39¼, 42, 43½, 46½, 48, 50, 52¼)"
Ribbing
19¾ (20½, 22¼, 23, 24¾, 25¾, 27½, 28¼, 29½, 30¾)"

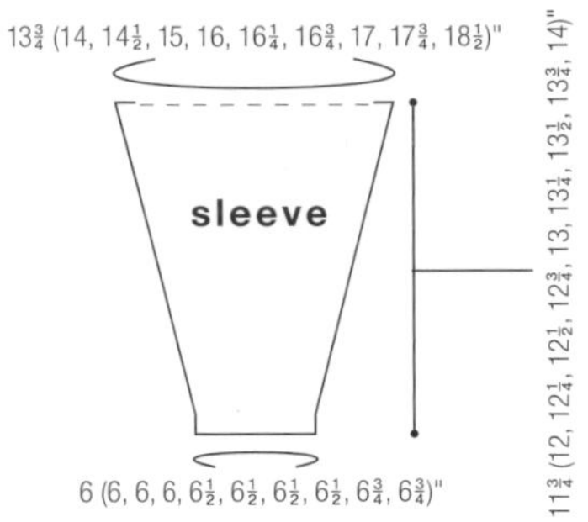

13¾ (14, 14½, 15, 16, 16¼, 16¾, 17, 17¾, 18½)"
sleeve
6 (6, 6, 6, 6½, 6½, 6½, 6½, 6¾, 6¾)"
11¾ (12, 12¼, 12½, 12¾, 13, 13¼, 13½, 13¾, 14)"

SUGARPLUM CHART

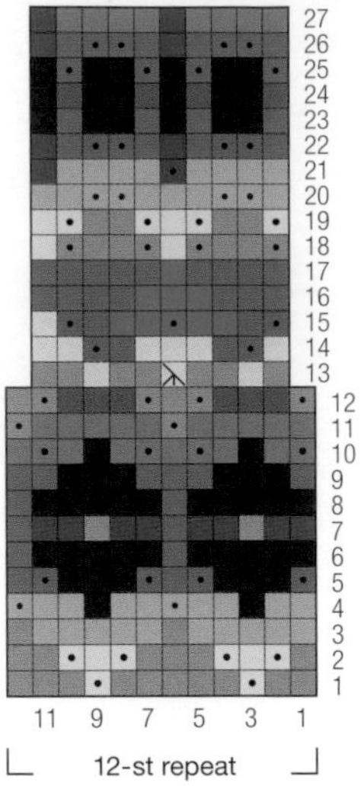

27
26
25
24
23
22
21
20
19
18
17
16
15
14
13
12
11
10
9
8
7
6
5
4
3
2
1
11 9 7 5 3 1
12-st repeat

COLOR KEY

- □ / ⊡ Knit / purl with color indicated
- light brown (MC)
- light green
- medium green
- dark green
- raspberry
- fuchsia
- orange
- copper
- silver gray
- turquoise
- Sk2p: Slip 1, k2tog, PSSO

Sweater

Body

Using turquoise, Tubular CO method (see Special Techniques, page 178), and smallest (size US 3) circ needle, CO 184 (192, 208, 216, 232, 240, 256, 264, 276, 288) sts. Join for working in the rnd, being careful not to twist sts; place marker (pm) for beginning of rnd.

Work 2 rnds Tubular St st (see Special Techniques, page 178).

Change to MC and size US 5 needle. Work one rnd in k1, p1 rib.

Establish Rib Pattern: * K1, RT-P, p1; repeat from * around.

Beginning with Rnd 1 of Cross-Stitch Rib, work even for 6 rnds.

Change to St st; work even for 0 (1, 2, 3, 4, 0, 1, 2, 3, 4) rnds.

Shape Waist: Pm for second side seam as follows: K92 (96, 104, 108, 116, 120, 128, 132, 138, 144), pm; knit to end of rnd.

Decrease Rnd: *Ssk, knit to 2 sts before next marker, k2tog; repeat from * once—4 sts decreased. Repeat decrease rnd every 6 (6, 6, 6, 6, 6, 8, 8, 8, 8) rnds 5 times—160 (168, 184, 192, 208, 216, 232, 240, 252, 264) sts remain.

Work 12 rnds even.

Increase Rnd: * K1, M1, knit around to one st before next marker, M1, k1; repeat from * once—4 sts increased. Repeat Increase Rnd every 6 (6, 6, 6, 6, 6, 8, 8, 8, 8) rnds 8 times—196 (204, 220, 228, 244, 252, 268, 276, 288, 300) sts.

Continuing in St st, work even until piece measures 12¼ (12½, 12¾, 13, 13¼, 13½, 13¾, 14, 14¼, 14¾)" from the beginning, ending last rnd 3 (3, 3, 3, 4, 4, 4, 4, 4, 5) sts before marker.

Divide for Front and Back

K6 (6, 6, 6, 8, 8, 8, 8, 8, 10) sts for left underarm, removing marker, place sts on holder; k39 (41, 43, 45, 46, 48, 50, 52, 54, 55) sts for left Front neck, pm; k14 (14, 18, 18, 22, 22, 26, 26, 28, 30) sts for center Front, pm; k39 (41, 43, 45, 46, 48, 50, 52, 54, 55) sts for right Front neck; k6 (6, 6, 6, 8, 8, 8, 8, 8, 10) sts for right underarm, removing marker, place sts on holder; k92 (96, 104, 108, 114, 118, 126, 130, 136, 140) sts for Back. Set aside, but do not break yarn.

Sleeves (make 2)

Using turquoise, Tubular CO method, and smallest (size US 3) dpn, CO 56 (56, 56, 56, 60, 60, 60, 60, 64, 64) sts. Join for working in the rnd, being careful not to twist sts; pm for beginning of rnd.

Work 2 rnds of Tubular St st.

Change to MC and size US 5 needles. Work 1 rnd k1, p1 rib.

Establish Rib Pattern: * K1, RT-P, p1; repeat from * around.
Beginning with Rnd 1 of Cross-Stitch Rib, work even for 12 rnds.
Change to St st; work even for 2 rnds.

Shape Sleeves: Increase 1 st each side of marker every 8 rows 10 (10, 3, 4, 2, 2, 0, 0, 0, 0) times, every 6 rows 0 (1, 9, 9, 12, 13, 14, 15, 15, 13) times; then every 4 rows 0 (0, 0, 0, 0, 0, 2, 2, 2, 6) times, as follows: K1, M1, knit around to one st before marker, M1, k1—2 sts increased—76 (78, 80, 82, 88, 90, 92, 94, 98, 102) sts.

Work even in St st until piece measures 11¾ (12, 12¼, 12½, 12¾, 13, 13¼, 13½, 13¾, 14)" from beginning, ending 3 (3, 3, 3, 4, 4, 4, 4, 4, 5) sts before marker.
Next Rnd: K6 (6, 6, 6, 8, 8, 8, 8, 8, 10) sts for underarm, place sts on holder; knit to end of rnd—70 (72, 74, 76, 80, 82, 84, 86, 90, 92) sts remain for sleeve. Break yarn and set aside.

Yoke

Using yarn attached to Body and US size 5 circ needle, k70 (72, 74, 76, 80, 82, 84, 86, 90, 92) sts of right Sleeve, pm for right Back raglan; k92 (96, 104, 108, 114, 118, 126, 130, 136, 140) Back sts, pm for left Back raglan; k70 (72, 74, 76, 80, 82, 84, 86, 90, 92) sts of left Sleeve, pm for left Front raglan; k92 (96, 104, 108, 114, 118, 126, 130, 136, 140) Front sts, slipping markers (sm) for neck, pm for right Front raglan—324 (336, 356, 368, 388, 400, 420, 432, 452, 464) sts total.

Begin Short Rows

Row 1: Knit to left Front neck marker, turn.
Row 2: Yo, purl to right Front neck marker, turn.
Row 3: Yo, * knit to 3 sts before next raglan marker, ssk, k1, sm, k1, k2tog; repeat from * 3 more times, knit to 3 sts before last left Front gap (not counting yo), turn—8 sts decreased.
Row 4: Yo, purl to 3 sts before last right Front gap, turn.

Repeat last 2 rows 7 (7, 8, 8, 9, 9, 10, 10, 11, 11) times—54 (56, 56, 58, 60, 62, 62, 64, 66, 68) sts remain each sleeve and 76 (80, 86, 90, 94, 98, 104, 108, 112, 116) sts remain each for Front and Back—260 (272, 284, 296, 308, 320, 332, 344, 356, 368) sts total.
Next Row: Yo, * knit to 3 sts before next raglan marker, ssk, k1, sm, k1, k2tog; repeat from * 3 more times, and AT THE SAME TIME, close all gaps formed by short rows by knitting the yo from the previous row together with the next st (as in k2tog)—52 (54, 54, 56, 58, 60, 60, 62, 64, 66) sts remain each sleeve and 74 (78, 84, 88, 92, 96, 102, 106, 110, 114) sts remain each for Front and Back—252 (264, 276, 288, 300, 312, 324, 336, 348, 360) sts total.
Next Row: Knit to right Back raglan marker—new beginning of rnd.

Establish Pattern: Change to largest (size US 7) circ needle and begin Sugarplum Chart; work Rnds 1–27 of chart, changing colors as indicated; decrease as indicated on Rnd 13—210 (220, 230, 240, 250, 260, 270, 280, 290, 300) sts remain.
Rnd 28: Change to size US 5 circ needle; * k2tog, p2, k1; repeat from * around— 168 (176, 184, 192, 200, 208, 216, 224, 232, 240) sts remain.
Change to Cross-Stitch rib; work even for 6 rnds, beginning with Rnd 2 (move marker one st to the right on the first rnd in order not to interrupt first 2 sts of pattern).
Next Rnd: * K1, RT-P, p1; repeat from * around.
Change to turquoise and smallest (size US 3) needle. Work 2 rnds of Tubular St st.
Rnd 1: * K1, slip 1 wyif; repeat from * around.
Rnd 2: * Slip 1 wyib, p1; repeat from * around.
Break yarn, leaving a tail 4 times as long as the neckline circumference.
BO all sts using Tubular BO method (see Special Techniques, page 177).

Finishing

Using yarn needle and Kitchener st (see Special Techniques, page 176), graft live sts of sleeves and body at underarms. Weave in all ends.
Block to finished measurements.

The winter solstice is an important date in northern climes, especially in Scandinavia, where entire days of darkness make people hunger for the return of light. Priscilla Gibson-Roberts found it appropriate, then, to take inspiration from the old folkwear shawls of Sweden and Finland—especially the "heart-warmer shawls," which, like this one, warm the heart (as well as the spirit) by wrapping around the back and shoulders, crisscrossing in the front, and then wrapping around once more before being tied.

The colors and patterning in this particular shawl also carry meaning for the winter solstice. The shawl is worked from the top down, first in a dark color called mountain twilight that signifies long, dark days. When the main field of color nears its end, the light returns in pale sunbursts, as it does at the end of winter. As the sun begins its long journey to the north, there is the promise of blue skies, the flowers of spring, and the long twilight to come.

FINISHED MEASUREMENTS
Approximately 84" by 25" without ties

YARN
Mountain Colors Bearfoot
(60% superwash wool / 25% mohair / 15% nylon; 350 yards / 100 grams):
2 skeins each mountain twilight, Yellowstone, and ruby river; 1 skein winter sky

NEEDLES
One 60" circular (circ) needle size US 1 (2.25 mm)
Two double-pointed needles size US 1 (2.25 mm)

NOTIONS
Crochet hook B/1 (2.25 mm), yarn needle

GAUGE
36 sts and 44 rows = 4" (10 cm) in Stockinette stitch (St st)

NOTES
✳ **Bobble:** [K1, p1, k1] in same st to increase to 3 sts, slip sts back onto left-hand needle, k3, slip sts back onto left-hand needle, slip 2 sts tog knitwise, k1, p2sso.

Shawl

Using mountain twilight, CO 6 sts through a loop, as follows: Make a circle of yarn around one or two fingers, leaving a 6" tail. Using a crochet hook and the strand of yarn attached to the ball, * insert hook into circle and pull up a loop (one stitch CO), yo hook (second stitch CO); repeat from * for number of stitches to be CO. Transfer stitches from hook to needle to be used for project; knit one row, working through the back loop of each stitch. Continue as instructed; after several rows have been worked, pull on tail to draw CO stitches together and close circle. Fasten tail securely. Purl 1 (WS) row.
Set-up Row (RS): K1-f/b in first st, k1, M1, k1, place marker (pm) for center; k1, M1, k1-f/b of next st, k1—4 sts increased.
Row 1: P1-f/b in first st, purl to last 2 sts, p1-f/b of next st, p1—2 sts increased.
Row 2: K1-f/b in first st, work to 1 st before marker, M1, k2, M1, work to last 2 sts, k1-f/b of next st, k1—4 sts increased. Repeat Rows 1 and 2 until there are 186 sts on each side of center marker, ending after finishing a WS row.

Continuing to shape sides and center by rpeating Rows 1 and 2, begin working Chart patterns in numerical order, beginning with Chart 1, changing colors as indicated. After all charts have been completed, BO with ruby red on the last row of Chart X.

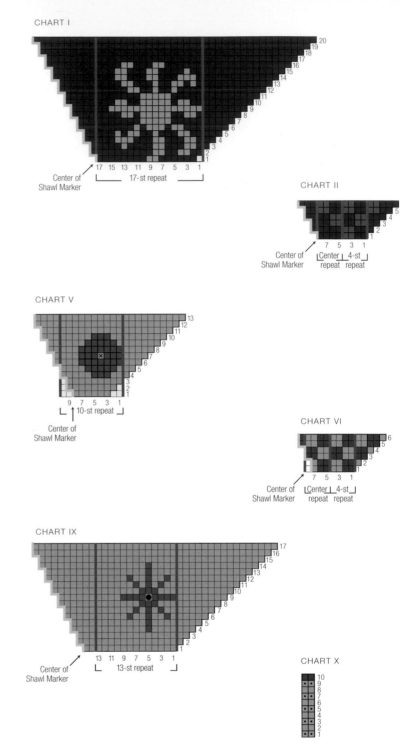

Edging

Using crochet hook and ruby red, work 1 row sc
evenly across shaped edges of shawl, skipping
Garter st rows; fasten off.

Join ruby red to BO edge, skipping Garter
st rows.

Work Shell pattern as follows: * Skip 2 sts, work
6 dc in next st, skip 2 sts, sc in next st; repeat
from * along both diagonal edges, working a
shell (6 dc) into point; end with a sc in last st
before Garter st rows; fasten off.

Ties

With RS facing, using dpn, pick up and knit 5
sts along the side in Garter st rows; work I-cord
(see Special Techniques, page 175) 24" long;
fasten off. Repeat on opposite side.

Finishing

In the center st of the motif Chart V (marked
with an X), make a 4-wrap bouillon embroidery
stitch for the flower center.

Make two 5" Tassels (see Special Techniques,
page 177) and attach to ends of I-cords. Weave
in all loose ends. Block lightly with steam.

CHART III

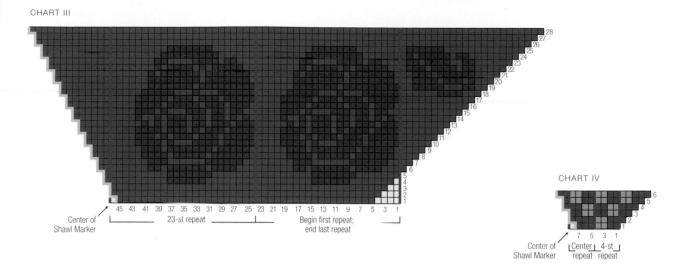

Center of Shawl Marker

45 43 41 39 37 35 33 31 29 27 25 23 21 19 17 15 13 11 9 7 5 3 1

23-st repeat

Begin first repeat; end last repeat

CHART IV

Center of Shawl Marker

7 5 3 1

Center repeat 4-st repeat

CHART VII

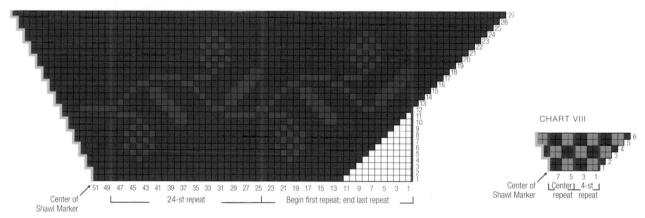

Center of Shawl Marker

51 49 47 45 43 41 39 37 35 33 31 29 27 25 23 21 19 17 15 13 11 9 7 5 3 1

24-st repeat

Begin first repeat; end last repeat

CHART VIII

Center of Shawl Marker

7 5 3 1

Center repeat 4-st repeat

CHART NOTES

1. Charts show right-hand edge and center marker edge; both edges continue to increase while Charts are being worked.

2. Read each row of all Charts from right to left until you reach the center marker (shown on Charts with a green line); then work the same row in reverse (from left to right).

3. Some Charts show 2 repeats because the repeat changes at the center marker; work to center marker, then work in reverse to right-hand edge of Chart as for other Charts.

4. Some Charts show areas where there are no stitches at the beginning (first repeat), or at the center marker (last repeat before reversing direction). For first repeat, begin with the first st in background color for repeat; then work no stitch areas with background color for remaining repeats until you reach the last background st at center marker (this may not be a full repeat, or it may be the beginning of an additional repeat as on Chart VII); reverse direction at the last Charted background st, and work to right-hand edge of Chart, ending last repeat at last Charted background st.

5. Work bobble in Chart X where indicated.

COLOR KEY

☐ St st: Knit on RS, purl on WS

⊡ Rev St st: Purl on RS, knit on WS

☐ No stitch: At beginning/end of row, work in background color for remaining repeats; at center marker, work in background color if part of repeat, then when center marker is reached, begin working from left to right from last stitch in background color.

■ mountain twilight

▨ St st: Yellowstone

⊡ Rev St st: Yellowstone

■ ruby river

■ winter sky

◉ Bobble

☒ Embroider 4-wrap Bouillon stitch

JOLENE TREACE *River Forest Gansey*

The stitch patterns in these ganseys—a Tree of Life motif and a basketweave stitch—echo JoLene Treace's childhood memories of her grandparents' log cabin, where her family would gather on New Year's Day for sledding, skating, and exploring the nearby woods. Her recollections of tromping through the woods, gathering treasures in baskets, and playing hard in the snow with her cousins are knitted into this warm, wooly sweater, sized so both you and a little one can create your own adventure-filled memories.

FINISHED MEASUREMENTS
To fit Child < Adult >
Chest: 25 (29, 33, 37)"; < 39 (43, 47, 51, 55)" >
Ganseys shown measure 29" < 47" >

YARN
Cascade 220 (100% wool; 220 yards /
3.5 ounces): 3 (4, 5, 6) skeins; < 7 (8, 9, 10, 11) >
skeins. Shown in #4010 heathered gold
< #9429 green >

NEEDLES
One 16" circular (circ) needle size US 5
(3.75 mm)
One 24" circular needle size US 7 (4.5 mm)
Change needle size if necessary to obtain
correct gauge.

NOTIONS
Stitch holders, stitch marker, yarn needle

GAUGE
24 sts and 32 rows = 4" (10 cm) in Pattern A
(first 4 rows of Chart)

NOTES
✳ The first and last stitches of each garment piece are selvage stitches (work in St st throughout). They are NOT charted, but are included in the st counts.
✳ All shaping should be done inside the selvage sts.

✳ **Pattern Stitches**
See Charts

Gansey

Back
Using smaller needle and Double-Strand CO method (see Special Techniques, page 174) or other elastic CO method of your choice, CO 75 (87, 99, 111); < 117 (129, 141, 153, 165) >; begin Garter st on all sts except first and last sts (selvage sts—work in St st throughout). Beginning with a WS row, work even for 8 rows, ending with a RS row.
Change to larger needle and Chart.

Establish Pattern: (WS) P1 (selvage st), begin Row 1, St 11 (5, 11, 5); < 1 (7, 1, 7, 1) > of Child <Adult> Gansey Chart, work 24-st repeat 3 (3, 4, 4); < 4 (5, 5, 6, 6) > times across, end st 35 (41, 35, 41); < 43 (37, 43, 37, 43) >, p1 (selvage st).
Continuing as established, work 4-row repeat of Pattern A 11 (15, 19, 21); < 23 (23, 23, 23, 23) > times, then work 4 Transition rows once. Begin Pattern B; work 8-row repeat 1 (1, 2, 2); < 2 > times, ending with RS row (Row 16).

Shape Armhole: (WS) BO 4 (4, 6, 6); < 6 (6, 6, 7, 8) > sts at beginning of next 2 rows—67 (79, 87, 99); < 105 (117, 129, 139, 149) > sts remain. (RS) Decrease 1 st each side this row, then every other row 3 (5, 6, 9) times; < 6 (7, 9, 9, 10) > times—61 (69, 75, 81); < 93 (103, 111, 121, 129) > sts remain. Continuing in Pattern B, work even until armhole measures 4 (4¾, 5¼, 6¼)"; < 6½, 7¼, 8, 8¾, 9½)" > from beginning of shaping, ending with a WS row.

Shape Shoulders and Neck: (RS) Work
19 (22, 24, 26); < 34 (37, 40, 43, 45) > sts; join
a second ball of yarn and BO 23 (25, 27, 29);
< 25 (29, 31, 35, 39 > sts for neck; work to end.
Working both sides at same time, work 1
row even.
(RS) At each neck edge, decrease 1 st this row,
then every other row 4; < 7 > times, working 1 st
in from each neck edge (selvage st), as follows:
On right Back, work across to 3 sts from neck
edge, k2tog, k1; on left Back, k1, ssk, work to
end—14 (17, 19, 21); < 26 (29, 32, 35, 37) > sts
remain each side for shoulders. Work even as es-
tablished until armhole measures $5\frac{1}{2}$ ($6\frac{1}{4}$, $6\frac{3}{4}$, $7\frac{3}{4}$)";
< $8\frac{1}{2}$ ($9\frac{1}{4}$, 10, $10\frac{3}{4}$, $11\frac{1}{2}$)" >, ending with a WS row;
place remaining sts on holders.

Front

Work as for Back until armhole measures
$2\frac{3}{4}$ ($3\frac{1}{2}$, $3\frac{1}{2}$, $4\frac{1}{2}$)"; < $4\frac{3}{4}$ ($5\frac{1}{2}$, $6\frac{1}{4}$, 7, $7\frac{3}{4}$)" > from
beginning of shaping, ending with a WS row—
61 (69, 75, 81); < 93 (103, 111, 121, 129) >
sts remain.

Shape Neck: (RS) Work 25 (29, 31, 34);
< 40 (44, 48, 52, 55) > sts; join a second ball of
yarn and BO 11 (11, 13, 13); < 13 (15, 15, 17, 19) >
sts for neck; work to end. Working both sides at
same time, work 1 row even.
(RS) All sizes: At neck edge, BO 2 sts at beginning of next 4 rows—21 (25, 27, 30); < 36 (40,
44, 48, 51) > sts remain each side for shoulder.
(RS) Decrease 1 st at each neck edge every
other row 7 (8, 8, 9); < 10 (11, 12, 13, 14) >
times—14 (17, 19, 21); < 26 (29, 32, 35, 37) >
sts remain for each shoulder. Work even until
armhole measures same as Back to shoulder;
place remaining sts on holders.

Sleeve (make 2)

*Note: Transition rows start before shaping
is complete for some children's sizes.*
Working as for Back, CO 41 (47, 51, 53);
< 55 (59, 63, 65, 69) > sts; begin Garter st.
Work even for 8 rows as for Back, ending
with a RS row.
Change to larger needle and Chart.

CHILD GANSEY CHART

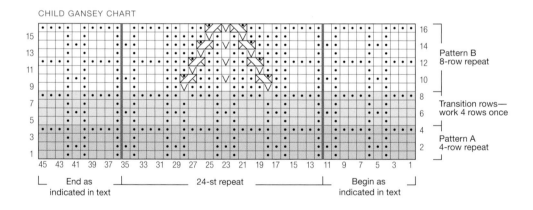

ADULT GANSEY CHART

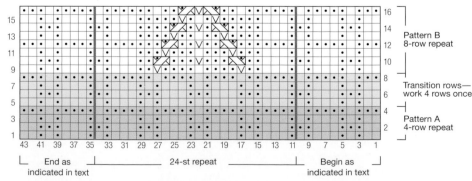

KEY

☐	Knit on RS, purl on WS
⊡	Purl on RS, knit on WS
☑	Slip 1 purlwise
⧄	Slip next st to cn, hold to front, p1, k1 from cn.
⧅	Slip next st to cn, hold to back, k1, p1 from cn.

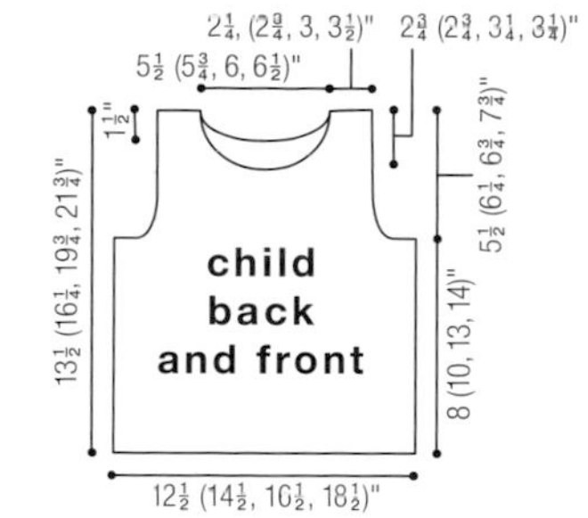

2¼, (2¾, 3, 3½)"
2¾ (2¾, 3¼, 3¼)"
5½ (5¾, 6, 6½)"
1½"
13½ (16¼, 19¾, 21¾)"
5½ (6¼, 6¾, 7¾)"
8 (10, 13, 14)"
child
back
and front
12½ (14½, 16½, 18½)"

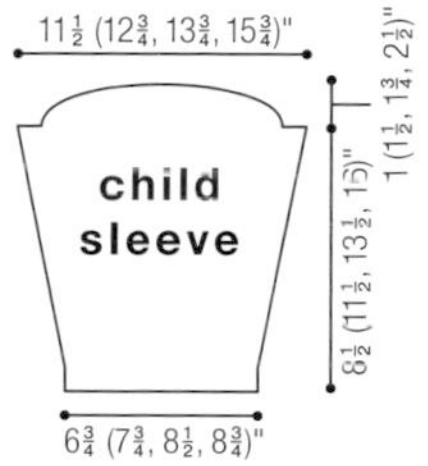

11½ (12¾, 13¾, 15¾)"
1 (1½, 1¾, 2½)"
child
sleeve
8½ (11¼, 13½, 15)"
6¾ (7¾, 8½, 8¾)"

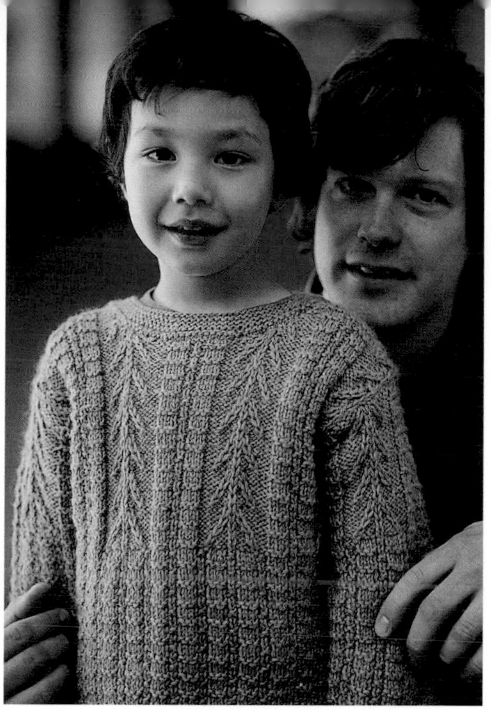

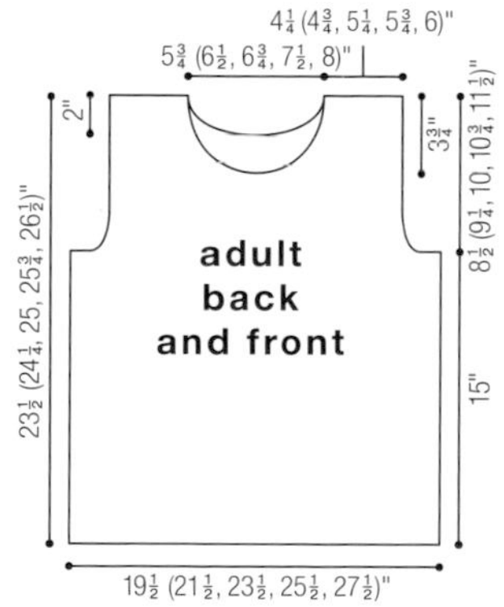

4¼ (4¾, 5¼, 5¾, 6)"
5¾ (6½, 6¾, 7½, 8)"
2"
3¾"
23½ (24¼, 25, 25¾, 26½)"
8½ (9¼, 10, 10¾, 11½)"
adult
back
and front
15"
19½ (21½, 23½, 25½, 27½)"

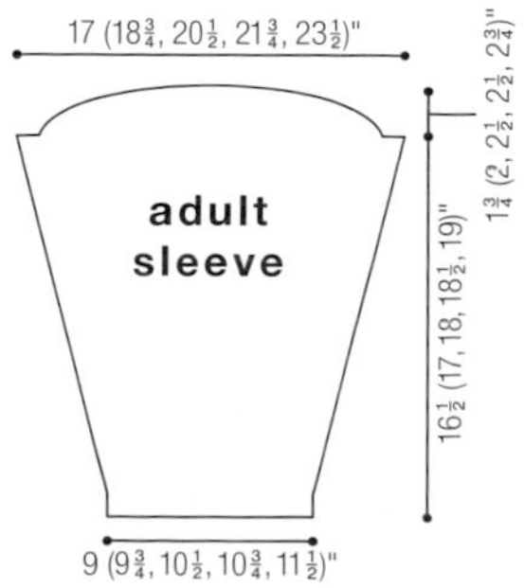

17 (18¾, 20½, 21¾, 23½)"
1¾ (2, 2½, 2½, 2¾)"
adult
sleeve
16½ (17, 18, 18½, 19)"
9 (9¾, 10½, 10¾, 11½)"

Establish Pattern: (WS) P1 (selvage st), begin Row 1, St 4 (1, 11, 10); < 8 (6, 4, 3, 1) > of Child < Adult > Gansey Chart, work 24-st repeat 1 (1, 2, 2); < 2 > times across, end St 42 (45, 35, 36); < 36 (38, 40, 41, 43) >, p1 (selvage st).
Continuing as established, work 4-row repeat of Pattern A 12 (18, 20, 25); < 26 (27, 29, 30, 31) > times, then work 4 Transition rows once.
Begin Pattern B; work 8-row repeat 1 (1, 2, 2); < 2 > times; and AT THE SAME TIME,

Shape Sleeve: Increase 1 st each side every 4; < 4 (4, 4, 2, 2) > rows 14 (6, 3, 10); < 17 (23, 29, 3, 7) > times, then every 6; < 6 (6, 6, 4, 4) > rows 0 (9, 13, 11); < 7 (4, 1, 30, 29) > times, working increased sts in pattern as they become available, as follows:
(RS) K1, M1, work across to last st, M1, k1—69 (77, 83, 95); < 103 (113, 123, 131, 141) > sts; ending with a WS row.

Shape Cap: (RS) Continuing as established, BO 4 (4, 6, 6); < 6 (6, 6, 7, 8) > sts at beg of next 2 rows—61 (69, 71, 83); < 91 (101, 111, 117, 125) > sts remain. Work 1 row even.
(RS) Decrease 1 st each side every other row 3 (5, 6, 9); < 6 (7, 9, 9, 10) > times—55 (59, 59, 65); < 79 (87, 93, 99, 105) > sts remain. Work 1 row even; BO remaining sts.

Finishing

Place shoulder sts from holders with RS together (WS out); join using 3-Needle BO method (see Special Techniques, page 177); fasten off. Set in sleeves, matching shaping; sew side and sleeve seams. Weave in ends.

Neckband

Using larger needle, beginning at left shoulder seam, pick up and knit 21 (22, 24, 25); < 27 (28, 29, 30, 31) > sts along left Front neck shaping; 11 (11, 13, 13); < 13 (15, 15, 17, 19) > sts at center Front; (21 (22, 24, 25); < 27 (28, 29, 30, 31) > sts along right Front neck shaping; 10; < 12 > sts along Back neck shaping; 23 (25, 27, 29); < 25 (29, 31, 35, 39) > sts at center Back; 10; < 12 > sts along Back neck shaping to left shoulder—96 (100, 108, 112); < 116 (124, 128, 136, 144) > sts. Join for working in the rnd; place marker (pm) for beginning of rnd.

Change to smaller needle and Garter st; beginning with a purl rnd, work 4 rnds even.

Shape Neckband:
Rnd 5: Decrease 4; < 6 > sts this rnd by p2tog at the following points:
At shoulder seams (adults only this rnd), and at each side of center Front and Back sts (where the center neck sts meet the side neck shaping sts)— 92 (96, 104, 108); < 110 (118, 122, 130, 138) > sts remain.
Rnd 6: Work even.
Rnd 7: Decrease 6; < 6 > sts this rnd at all points given Rnd 5—86 (90, 98, 102); < 104 (112, 116, 124, 132) > sts remain.
Rnd 8: Work even.
BO all sts loosely as if to purl. Weave in ends. Wash and block to measurements.

BETTY CHRISTIANSEN *Cardinal Joy Hoodie*

Nothing brings joy to the holiday season like a child—celebrate yours with this adorable hoodie that declares what the season is all about (in French or English, as you wish). It's generously sized to ensure long wearabilty and features many fun-to-knit details—hemmed edges, a tasseled "tomten" hood, and a kangaroo pocket with a cardinal motif. A shy winter bird, the cardinal makes its presence known as a bright flash of red against the snow and by its song, a particularly joyful version of which is heard high in the treetops near the end of winter, welcoming spring and the ever-warming sunshine on its feathers. As such, the cardinal captures the true spirit of the solstice—proclaiming its faith in light and warmth even as it abides the winter.

FINISHED MEASUREMENTS
25 (28½, 32)" chest
Hoodie shown measures 25"

YARN
Goddess Yarns Emanuella (100% merino wool; 90 yards / 50 grams): 6 (7, 8) skeins MC; 1 skein each A, B, C, and D
Shown in the following colors: #1350 copper (MC), #1374 brown (A), #6085 red (B), #0713 gold (C), #50 black (D)

NEEDLES
One pair straight needles size US 6 (4 mm)
One pair straight needles size US 7 (4.5 mm)
Change needle size if necessary to obtain correct gauge.

NOTIONS
Stitch holders (or waste yarn), yarn needle

GAUGE
18 sts and 24 rows = 4" (10 cm) in St st using larger needles

Hoodie

Back

Using smaller needles and MC, CO 56 (64, 72) sts; begin St st.
Hem Facing: Work even for 6 rows, ending with a WS row.
(RS) Join A; knit 1 row.
(WS) Change to larger needles; knit 1 row (contrast turning ridge); break A.
Continuing with larger needles, MC and St st, work even until piece measures 6½ (7¾, 9)" from turning ridge, ending with a WS row.

Shape Raglan Armhole: Decrease 1 st each side this row, then every other row 16 (18, 20) times as follows: (RS) K2, k2tog, knit across to last 4 sts, ssk, k2. Work 1 row even—22 (26, 30) sts remain for neck; BO all sts.

Front

Work as for Back until piece measures 1" above turning row, ending with a WS row.

Pocket Lining: (RS) K10 (12, 14); place next 36 (40, 44) sts on a holder for Pocket; CO 36 (40, 44) sts for Pocket lining, knit to end. Work even as established for 30 (34, 38) rows, ending with a WS row; place all sts on a holder.

Pocket: Place the 36 (40, 44) Pocket sts from holder on needle; join A. Knit 2 rows. Join MC and begin Pocket Chart. Work 28 (32, 36) rows as indicated for your size, using separate balls of yarn for each color, Intarsia method (see Special Techniques, page 175); work one Rev St st one st in from each edge, and work decrease 2 sts in from each edge as shown for smallest size—26 (30, 32) sts remain. Join A; knit 2 rows. Place sts on a holder.

Sew lower edge of Pocket closed by sewing the CO edge of the lining to the WS of pocket on the row just before the contrast color (A) ridge. Work the embroidery as indicated on the chart, working letters (in French or English) with A, feet with D and beak lines and eye with C.

POCKET CHART

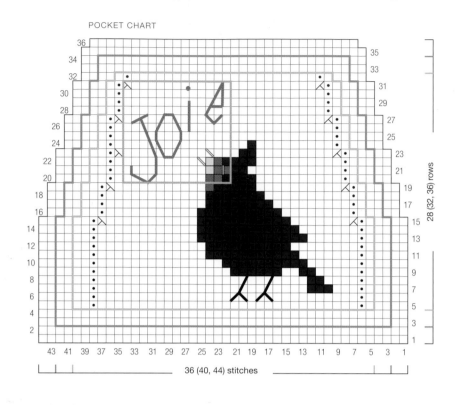

28 (32, 36) rows

36 (40, 44) stitches

POCKET INSERT CHART

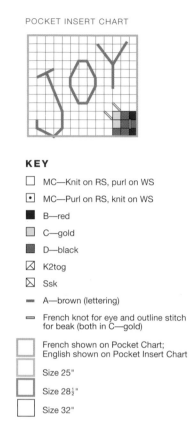

KEY

☐ MC—Knit on RS, purl on WS

▫ MC—Purl on RS, knit on WS

◼ B—red

◻ C—gold

◼ D—black

⊠ K2tog

⊠ Ssk

— A—brown (lettering)

= French knot for eye and outline stitch for beak (both in C—gold)

☐ French shown on Pocket Chart; English shown on Pocket Insert Chart

☐ Size 25"

☐ Size 28½"

☐ Size 32"

Join Pocket: Place the Front sts from holder on needle; using MC, join Pocket to Front as follows: K15 (17, 20) sts from Front; place Pocket sts on holder on top of Front sts, with WS of Pocket facing RS of Front; knit 26 (30, 32) Pocket sts together with next 26 (30, 32) sts of Front; knit remaining 15 (17, 20) sts of Front.
Continue as established in St st until Front measures 6½ (7¾, 9)" from turning ridge, ending with a WS row.

Shape Raglan Armhole: Work as for Back until 34 (38, 42) sts remain, ending with a WS row.

Shape Neck: Continuing armhole shaping as for Back, work as follows:
Row 1 (RS): K2, k2tog, k6, ssk, k1; join a second ball of yarn and BO 8 (12, 16) sts for neck (stitch left on needle counts as k1), k2tog, k6, ssk, k2—11 sts remain for each side.
Row 2: Working both sides at same time, purl.
Row 3: K2, k2tog, knit to 3 sts before neck edge, ssk, k1; on other neck edge, k1, k2tog, knit to last 4 sts, ssk, k2.

Row 4: Purl.
Repeat Rows 3 and 4 until 5 sts remain each side, ending with Row 4 (WS row).
Next Decrease Row: K2, k2tog, k1; on other side, k1, ssk, k2—4 sts remain each side.
Purl 1 row.
Final Decrease: K2, k2tog; on other side, ssk, k2—3 sts remain each side.
Purl 1 row; BO all sts.

Sleeve (make 2)
Using smaller needles and MC, CO 34 (37, 40) sts; begin St st.
Hem Facing: Work even for 4 rows, ending with a WS row.
(RS) Join A; knit 1 row.
(WS) Change to larger needles; knit 1 row (contrast turning ridge); break A.
Continuing with larger needles, MC and St st, work even for 6 rows, ending with a WS row.

Shape Sleeve: Increase 1 st each side this row, then every 6 rows 5 (6, 7) times—46 (51, 56) sts. Work even until piece measures 7½ (8¾, 10)" from turning ridge, ending with a WS row.

Shape Hood: BO 11 (12, 12) sts at beginning of next 4 rows—22 (22, 26) sts remain. BO remaining sts.

Finishing

Sew sleeves to Front and Back along raglan edges; sew sleeve and side seams.

Hem: On all pieces except Hood, fold hem to WS at turning ridge; stitch CO edge to WS of work.

Hood: Fold Hood in half; sew center Back seam. Sew Hood to neck edge, being careful to match Hood seam with center Back of sweater and ends with center Front; the decreased section of the Hood fits along the Front neck shaping. Leave the hem facing open; then go back and stitch the facing in place, enclosing the neck seam as you do so. Weave in ends. Block to measurements.

Tassel: Using A, make Tassel (see Special Techniques, page 177) and attach to tip of Hood.

Shape Raglan Armhole: Decrease 1 st each side this row, then every other row 16 (18, 20) times as follows: (RS) K2, k2tog, knit across to last 4 sts, ssk, k2. Work 1 row even—12 (13, 14) sts remain; BO all sts.

Hood

Using smaller needles and MC, CO 80 (84, 88) sts; begin St st.

Hem Facing: Work even for 2 rows, ending with a WS row.

Rows 3 and 5 (RS): Knit, increasing 1 st each side—82 (86, 90) sts.

Rows 4 and 6: Purl—84 (88, 92) sts.

Row 7: Join A; work as for Row 3—86 (90, 94) sts.

Row 8: Change to larger needles; knit 1 row (contrast turning ridge); break A.

Continuing with larger needles, MC and St st, work even for 2 rows, ending with a WS row.

Row 11: Knit, decreasing 1 st each side—84 (88, 92) sts remain.

Row 12: Purl.

Repeat Rows 11 and 12 until 66 (70, 74) sts remain, then work even until piece measures 5 (5¾, 6½)" from last decrease row, ending with a WS row.

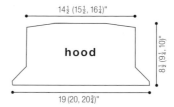

hood

14½ (15½, 16¼)"

8½ (9¼, 10)"

19 (20, 20¾)"

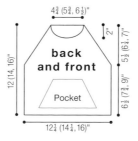

back and front

Pocket

4¾ (5¾, 6½)"

2"

5½ (6¼, 7)"

6½ (7¾, 9)"

12 (14, 16)"

12¼ (14¼, 16)"

sleeve

10 (11¼, 12¼)"

5½ (6¼, 7)"

7½ (8¾, 10)"

7½ (8, 8¾)"

JOLENE TREACE
Evergreen Shawl

When all other trees have gone dormant for the season, evergreens hold a silent vigil. It's no wonder, then, that evergreens—pine trees, spruce trees, and holly—have become sacred symbols of the winter holidays, honored and even worshiped in many cultures for centuries. This timeless shawl, inspired by a visit to the eclectic, artsy, and tree-filled town of New Harmony, Indiana, is worthy of honor too. With pinecone and leaf motifs worked into its lace pattern, it's a beautiful, slightly earthy, but totally contemporary accessory that can be wrapped around the shoulders like a traditional shawl or tossed around the neck over a vintage coat like a casual scarf.

FINISHED MEASUREMENTS
$63\frac{1}{2}$" wide across the top by 45" along the diagonal sides

YARN
Black Water Abbey $\frac{2}{8}$ Organic (100% wool; 330 yards / 2.5 ounces): 3 skeins olive

NEEDLES
Two 32" circular needles size US 6 (4 mm)
One 32" circular needle size US 10 (6 mm)
One set of five double-pointed needles size US 6 (4 mm)
Change needle size if necessary to obtain correct gauge.

NOTIONS
Stitch markers, yarn needle

GAUGE
12-stitch repeat = $2\frac{3}{4}$" using smaller needles after blocking; exact gauge is not essential

NOTES
* A Provisional CO is used for the Border as the Edging is attached to live stitches as it is worked around.
* The stitch count at CO includes 2 selvage sts that are not charted.
* The Border Chart represents one diagonal edge of the shawl, labeled A, B and C; these letters correspond to the letters on the schematic. Work each row across to the center stitch, then work it again for the second diagonal section; do not work center decrease on second repeat; knit the last st.
* The shawl is shaped by decreasing to form the right, center, and left points, while working the border rows.
* Shaping at right and left points is worked by slipping the first stitch as if to knit on each row. Once slipped, it is not worked again until the edging is attached to the shawl.
* The center (triangular area marked D on the schematic) is worked from the center stitch up. Border stitches brought into work each row increase the width of the center as rows are worked.
* A set-up round is worked and then the Edging is attached to the live stitches from the set-up round.

Shawl

Border
Using larger needle and Provisional CO (see Special Techniques, page 176), CO 431 sts; purl 1 row.
Change to smaller needle; begin Row 1 of Border Chart as follows:
(RS) Slip first st as if to knit (selvage st), place marker (pm), * work 47 sts of Section A once; work 12-st repeat of Section B 10 times; work Section C to center point, + work center point decrease and pm on center st; repeat from * once, end at +, knit last st, turn.
(WS) Slip first st as if to knit, pm, purl across to marker at opposite end (one st left unworked), turn.

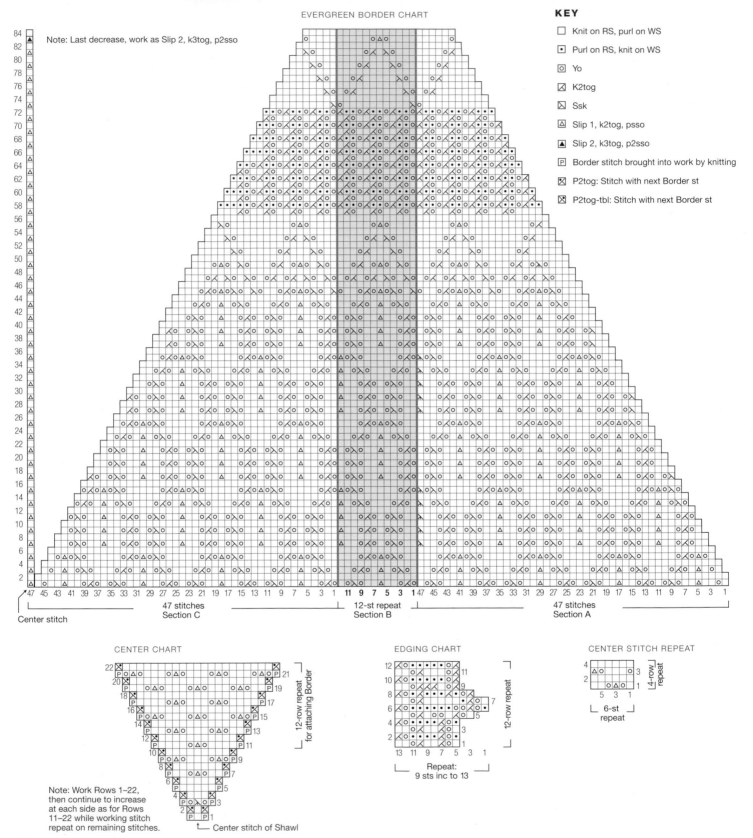

EVERGREEN BORDER CHART

KEY

☐ Knit on RS, purl on WS

⊡ Purl on RS, knit on WS

⊙ Yo

◺ K2tog

◹ Ssk

△ Slip 1, k2tog, psso

▲ Slip 2, k3tog, p2sso

Ⓟ Border stitch brought into work by knitting

⊠ P2tog: Stitch with next Border st

⊠ P2tog-tbl: Stitch with next Border st

Note: Last decrease, work as Slip 2, k3tog, p2sso

Center stitch

47 stitches
Section C

12-st repeat
Section B

47 stitches
Section A

CENTER CHART

12-row repeat
for attaching Border

Note: Work Rows 1–22,
then continue to increase
at each side as for Rows
11–22 while working stitch
repeat on remaining stitches.

Center stitch of Shawl

EDGING CHART

12-row repeat

Repeat:
9 sts inc to 13

CENTER STITCH REPEAT

4-row
repeat

6-st
repeat

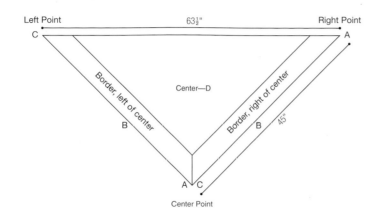

Left Point   63½"   Right Point

C   A

Border, left of center

Center—D

Border, right of center

B   B   45"

A C

Center Point

Moving markers at the end of each row as you come to them and replacing them one stitch further from the edge (after slipping the first st), continue as established until Border Chart is completed. (The number of stitches on hold at the right point will increase by 1 on RS rows and by 1 at left point on WS rows.)

Note: On Row 83 of Border Chart last center point decrease is worked as given.

On final row of the chart, leave the markers between the sts placed on hold for the right and left points and the remaining sts; pm on either side of center stitch. Break the yarn, leaving a tail long enough to weave in.

Center Section

Slip all sts to the right of the center st onto a second needle of the same size. The right-hand needle has the right point shaping sts (slipped sts) and the right border sts. The left-hand needle has the center st (where the center decrease for the center point was worked each row), the left border sts, and the left point shaping sts (slipped sts).

With RS facing, slip 1 st from the right-hand needle to the left-hand needle; the center pattern begins with the center st.

Beginning with Row 1 of Center Chart, work as indicated, bringing sts into work on each row from the Border stitches on either side of the center sts.

Continue as established, adding stitch repeats as sts are brought into work, until all border sts have been used.

Work 1 WS row; do not turn.

Set-Up Round

Continuing in the same direction, work set-up round for edging as follows:

Knit across the sts for the right point, increasing evenly to 54 sts, including the corner st, pm; knit sts from Provisional CO along right diagonal edge, increasing 1 st next to the center st, pm; knit the center st and remaining 215 sts from the Provisional CO along left diagonal edge, pm— (432 sts along the CO edge; 216 sts at each diagonal edge); knit across the left point sts, increasing evenly to 54 sts; knit across Center sts of Section D, increasing evenly to 189 sts— 297 sts across top of shawl, including 54 sts each side for the points. Do not break yarn.

Edging

Turn and begin working the Edging. Using a dpn the same size as the circular needle being used for the shawl and Knit-On CO method (see Special Techniques, page 176), CO 9 sts using the dpn for the right-hand needle and the circular needle for the left-hand needle.

Row 1 of Edging Chart (RS): Work across to last Edging st; work the last edging st together with the first shawl st on the left-hand needle by ssk; turn.

Row 2: Work from Chart.

Row 3: Work across to last Edging st; work the last edging st together with the next 2 shawl sts on left-hand needle by sk2p.

Row 4: Work from Chart.

Continue following Chart for all rows, attaching at the end of RS rows, alternating between ssk and sk2p as given for Rows 1 and 3 above. When attaching Edging at right and left point, work Rows 11 and 12 without attaching to the shawl—this will ease the edging around the point. There will be 33 points across the top of the shawl, and 24 points along each diagonal edge when Edging is completed. After the final WS row is worked, using a second dpn, pick up 9 sts along the edge of the knitted CO; graft the beginning and end of the edging together using Kitchener st (see Special Techniques, page 176). Weave in all ends.

CYNTHIA CRESCENZO

Wisconsin Winter Stole

When Cynthia Crescenzo spied Great Adirondack Yarn Company's Sequins—a marvelous hand-dyed yarn with an incredible drape and tiny sequins woven right in—she couldn't wait to see how it would look in a long, flowing fringe on a shawl knit with Kiki, an alpaca, silk, and merino blend yarn dyed-to-match. As Mary Veldy, who knit the sample stole for this book, worked with the yarn, she was reminded of winters in her western Wisconsin home. In the pale winter sunlight, she says, the snow sparkles and bare trees cast pearl-gray shadows, creating a mood that is at once calm and exhilarating.

FINISHED MEASUREMENTS
$15\frac{1}{2}$" wide by 61" long, excluding fringe

YARN
Great Adirondack Kiki (50% alpaca / 30% silk / 20% merino; 250 yards / 100 grams): 5 skeins Irish cream (MC)
Great Adirondack Sequins (90% rayon / 10% polyester; 100 yds / 43 grams): 4 skeins Irish cream (CC)

NEEDLES
One pair straight needles size US 5 (3.75 mm) needles
Change needle size if necessary to obtain correct gauge.

NOTIONS
Crochet hook size US F/5 (3.75 mm) for fringe
Stitch markers, cable needle (cn), yarn needle

GAUGE
30 sts (4 cables) and 32 rows = 4" (10 cm) in Cable pattern

NOTES
✢ **Edge Pattern**
(9 stitches each side of shawl) (see Chart)

✢ **Cable Pattern**
(multiple of 8 sts + 2; 24-row repeat) (see Chart)

Stole

Using MC, CO on 116 sts.

Establish pattern
(WS) Beginning Row 1 of Charts, work Edge Chart across first 9 sts; place marker (pm); work Cable Chart across center 98 sts, pm; work Edge Chart across remaining 9 sts.

Continuing as established, repeat Rows 1 and 2 of Edge Chart on first and last 9 sts, Rows 1–24 of Cable Chart on center sts, for remainder of piece. Work even until 480 rows total have been worked, ending Row 24 of Cable Chart. Continuing Edge Chart as established, work Rows 1–7 of Cable Chart on center sts once more; BO all sts loosely in pattern.

Fringe

For each Fringe, cut five strands of CC 20" long—500 strands total (50 Fringes per side).

Note: An easy way to do this, which takes advantage of the unique color patterning of this particular yarn, is to unwind a skein and lay it flat; decide which color you'd like featured on the stole end of the fringe (here, we've chosen white), and lay the skein so those portions of color are centered at either end. Now, simply cut the skein in half across the center, separate the strands into sets of five, and fold them in half; your "featured color" should be at the center of the fold.

Attach Fringe (see Special Techniques, page 175) to CO and BO edges, approximately every $\frac{1}{4}$".

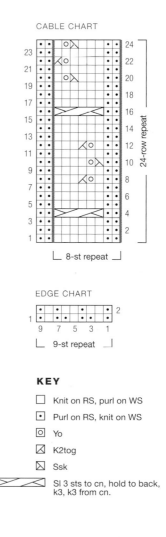

CABLE CHART

8-st repeat

24-row repeat

EDGE CHART

9-st repeat

KEY

☐	Knit on RS, purl on WS
•	Purl on RS, knit on WS
⊡	Yo
⊠	K2tog
⊠	Ssk
⟋⟍	Sl 3 sts to cn, hold to back, k3, k3 from cn.

This lace-patterned cashmere camisole was inspired by the handwork Nancy Meir Minsky found in a lace shop at *La Grand Place*, a marketplace in the center of old Brussels. Slip into it for a sophisticated statement at a holiday cocktail party or a subtly sexy look on New Year's Eve.

FINISHED MEASUREMENTS
32 (35, 38, 41)" chest
Camisole shown measures 38"

YARN
Classic Elite Charmed (85% cashmere / 15% mohair; 130 yards / 50 grams): 3 (3, 3, 4) balls #76708 heathered rose

NEEDLES
One pair straight needles size US 6 (4 mm)
One pair straight needles size US 7 (4.5 mm)
Change needle size if necessary to obtain correct gauge.

NOTIONS
Stitch holders, yarn needle

GAUGE
14 sts and 23 rows = 3" (7.6 cm) in Lace pattern

NOTES
✢ **Lace Pattern**
(multiple of 7 stitches plus 5; 2-row repeat)
Row 1 (WS): P5, * k2, p5; repeat from * to end.
Row 2 (RS): K2, slip 1 wyib, k2, * p2, k2, slip 1 wyib, k2; repeat from * to end.
Row 3: P5, * yo, p2tog, p5; repeat from * to end.
Row 4: K2, slip 1 wyib, k2, * yo, skp, k2, slip 1 wyib, k2; repeat from * to end.
Repeat Rows 3 and 4 for Lace pattern.

Camisole

Back

Using smaller needles, CO 75 (82, 89, 96) sts; begin Lace pattern. Work even for 9 rows, ending with a WS row. Change to larger needles.

Shape Sides: (RS) * Continuing as established, k1, skp, work across to last 3 sts, k2tog, k1—73 (80, 87, 94) sts remain. Work even for 7 rows. Repeat from * 3 times—67 (74, 81, 88) sts. Work even for 7 more rows.
* Next Row: K2, M1, work across to last 2 sts, M1, k2—69 (76, 83, 90) sts. Work even for 7 rows. Repeat from * 3 times, working inc sts into pattern—75 (82, 89, 96) sts.

Work even in Lace pattern until piece measures 12½ (13, 13, 13)" from the beginning, ending with a RS row.
Next Row: (WS) Work across in pattern, working [yo, p1] in center st for sizes 32 and 38 only—76 (82, 90, 96) sts.

Shape Right Back Armhole and Neck
Note: Before beginning shaping, make sure you will have enough yarn to finish the piece without any joins. Do not work yo without a corresponding decrease.
Row 1 (RS): BO 3 (4, 5, 6) sts for armhole (one st on right-hand needle), work 33 (35, 38, 40) sts as established, slip 1 st—35 (37, 40, 42) sts on right-hand needle; place rem 38 (41, 45, 48) sts on holder for left back.
Row 2: At neck edge, p2tog, BO 1 st, work to end—33 (35, 38, 40) sts remain.
Row 3: K2tog, BO 2 (2, 3, 3) sts for armhole, work across to last st, slip 1—30 (32, 34, 36) sts remain.
Row 4: At neck edge, p2tog, BO 7 (9, 9, 11) sts; work to end—22 (22, 24, 24) sts remain.
Row 5: K2tog, work across to last st, slip 1—21 (21, 23, 23) sts remain.
Row 6: At neck edge, p2tog, BO 3 (3, 5, 5) sts, work to end—17 sts remain.
Row 7: K2tog, work across to last st, slip 1—16 sts remain.
Row 8: At neck edge, p2tog, BO 1 st, work to end—14 sts remain.

Repeat Rows 7 and 8 two times, then work Row 7 once more, ending with a RS row—7 sts remain.

Strap

Next row (WS): * P1, yo, p2tog; repeat from *
2 times, p1.
Next row (RS): * K1, yo, skp; repeat from *
2 times, k1.
Repeat last two rows until armhole measures
6½ (7, 7½, 8)" from beginning of shaping;
place remaining sts on holder.

Shape Left Back Armhole and Neck

With WS facing, place left Back sts on needle;
join yarn at armhole edge, ready to work a
WS row.
Row 1 (WS): BO 3 (4, 5, 6) sts for armhole (one
st on right-hand needle), work 33 (35, 38, 40)
sts, slip 1—35 (37, 40, 42) sts.
Row 2: At neck edge, skp, BO 1 st, work to
end—33 (35, 38, 40) sts remain.
Row 3: P2tog, BO 2 (2, 3, 3) sts for armhole,
work across to last st, slip 1—30 (32, 34, 36)
sts remain.
Row 4: At neck edge, skp, BO 7 (9, 9, 11) sts,
work to end—22 (22, 24, 24) sts remain.
Row 5: P2tog, work across to last st, slip 1—
21 (21, 23, 23) sts remain.
Row 6: At neck edge, skp, BO 3 (3, 5, 5) sts,
work to end—17 sts remain.
Row 7: P2tog, work across to last st, slip 1—
16 sts remain.
Row 8: At neck edge, skp, BO 1 st, work to
end—14 sts remain.
Repeat Rows 7 and 8 two times, then work
Row 7 once more, ending with a WS row—
7 sts remain.

Strap

Next row (RS): * K1, yo, skp; repeat from *
2 times, k1.
Next row (WS): * P1, yo, p2tog; repeat from *
2 times, p1.
Work to match right Back Strap.

Front

Work as for Back until piece measures
11 (11½, 11½, 11½)" from the beginning, ending
with a WS row.

Left Front

Row 1 (RS): Work 37 (40, 44, 47) sts as
established, slip next st; place remaining
38 (41, 45, 48) sts on holder for right Front.
Row 2: P2tog, work to end—37 (40, 44, 47) sts.
Rows 3-12: Work even as established; piece
should measure same as Back to underarm.

Shape Left Front Armhole and Neck

Row 1 (RS): BO 3 (4, 5, 6) sts for armhole
(one st on right-hand needle), work 33 (35, 38,
40) sts, slip 1 st—34 (36, 39, 41) sts remain.
Row 2: At neck edge, p2tog, work to end—
33 (35, 38, 40) sts remain.
Work remainder of left Front as for right Back,
beginning with Row 3.

Right Front

With RS facing, place right Front sts on needle,
join yarn, work to end.
Row 1 (WS): Work 37 (40, 44, 47) sts as
established, slip next st.
Row 2: Skp, work to end—37 (40, 44, 47)
sts remain.
Rows 3–12: Work even as established; piece
should measure same as Back to underarm.

Shape Right Front Armhole and Neck

Row 1 (WS): BO 3 (4, 5, 6) sts for armhole (one
st on right-hand needle), work 33 (35, 38, 40)
sts, slip 1—34 (36, 39, 41) sts.
Row 2: At neck edge, skp, work to end—
33 (35, 38, 40) sts.
Work remainder of right Front as for left Back,
beginning with Row 3.

Finishing

Using a damp cloth, gently steam-block pieces
to finished measurements, and smooth out
edges. Sew side seams and try on garment;
adjust length of strap if necessary, by adding or
removing a few rows, then either graft live sts
or BO sts and sew seam. Weave in all ends,
tightening sts at center Back neck and Front
slit if necessary.

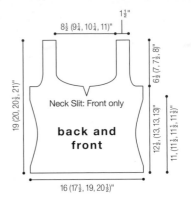

8½ (9¼, 10¼, 11)"
1½"
6½ (7, 7½, 8)"
19 (20, 20½, 21)"
Neck Slit: Front only
back and front
12½ (13, 13, 13)"
11, (11½, 11½, 11½)"
16 (17½, 19, 20½)"

PACKING UP

Carryalls, Gift Bags, and Last-Minute Gifts

Flower Pins/Package Decorations

Dress up yourself or a package with these pretty flowers. They're quick to make and are a great way to put leftover bits of yarn to good use. For package tying, consider coordinating the flower with twisted cord or I-cord. For wearing, attach a safety pin or a pin back to the back of the flower. The poppy flower shown here and the assortment of flowers on page 175 were all knitted with yarn left over from projects in this book. The look of the flowers can vary greatly depending on the character of the yarn with which they are made. Gauge isn't crucial. Choose a needle size based on the yarn you select.

Pinwheel Flower

First Point: CO 2 sts. Knit 1 row.
Shape First Point and Start Four More:
Continuing in Garter st, knit every row, increasing 1 st at the beginning of each row until there are 11 sts; break yarn.
* On the same needle, CO 2 sts for next Point. Work as for first point. Repeat from * 3 times—5 Points total. Do not break yarn on last Point.
Joining Row: Knit across all 5 Points—55 sts. Knit 2 rows even.
Shape Flower: * K2tog; repeat from * to last st, k1—28 sts remain.
Next Row: * K2tog; repeat from * across—14 sts remain.
Next Row: * K2tog; repeat from * across—7 sts remain.
Pass 6 sts over first st—1 st remains. Break yarn, thread through remaining st, and fasten off. Sew seam and weave in ends. Sew Bobble or beads to center of Flower.

Bobble

CO 1 st, leaving 6" tail
Row 1: [K1-f/b twice, k1] in same st—5 sts.
Row 2: K5.
Row 3: P5.
Pass 4 sts over first st—1 st remains. Break yarn, thread through remaining st, and secure.

Scallop Flower

First Scallop: CO 5 sts; begin Garter st.
Shape First Scallop and Start Four More:
Knitting every row, increase 1 st at the beginning of each row until there are 9 sts; break yarn.
* On the same needle, CO 5 sts for next Scallop. Work as for first scallop. Repeat from * 3 times—5 Scallops total. Do not break yarn on last Scallop.
Joining Row: Knit across all 5 Scallops—45 sts.
Shape Flower: * K2tog; repeat from * to last st, k1—23 sts remain.
Next row: * K2tog; repeat from * to last st, k1—12 sts remain.
Next Row: * K2tog; repeat from * across—6 sts remain.
Break yarn, thread through remaining sts, draw tight, and fasten securely. Sew seam. Weave in ends.

Double Pinwheel Flower

Make a Pinwheel Flower, a Scallop Flower, and a Bobble (see above).

Assemble: Stack a Scallop Flower on top of a pinwheel flower, then thread one tail of bobble through the centers of both Flowers. Thread the other tail through another space near the center and tie the two tails together in back to hold all parts in place.

Poppy Flower

Large Petal (make 5)
CO 3 sts.
Row 1: Knit.
Rows 2, 4, 6, 8, 10, 12, and 14: Purl.
Row 3: * K1, CO 1; rep from * to last st, k1—5 sts.
Row 5: Repeat Row 3—9 sts.
Row 7: Knit.
Row 9: Repeat Row 3—17 sts.
Rows 11 and 13: * Ssk, knit to last 2 sts, k2tog—13 sts remain after Row 13.
Row 15: Ssk, BO across to last 2 sts, k2tog, BO.
Break yarn, thread through remaining st, and fasten off.

Small Petal (make 3)
Work Rows 1–10 of Large Petal, then Row 15.

Join Petals: With a CO tail threaded on yarn needle, pick up loops of CO edge and gather all 5 Large Petals together. With same yarn, join the 3 Small Petals together in the same way and fasten securely to center of Large Petal group. Work 7 French knots, or sew beads in center, if desired.

Morning Star Flower

CO 55 sts.
Row 1 (RS): Purl.
Row 2: Knit.
Rows 3 and 5: [K2tog, k3, yo, k1, yo, k3, k2tog] 5 times.
Rows 4 and 6: Purl.
Row 7: * K3tog: repeat from * to last st, k1—19 sts remain.
Row 8: * P3tog; repeat from * to last st, p1—7 sts remain.
Row 9: * K2tog; repeat from * to last st, k1—4 sts remain.
Break yarn, leaving a 12" tail; thread tail through remaining sts on needle. Gather together and fasten off securely. Sew seam. Make a Bobble (see page 152) and fasten to center.

KIM HAMLIN
Balsam Sachets

If you've ever been to Maine, you might remember the small balsam sachets—commonly printed with trees, moose, or lighthouses—found in almost every gift shop. A native of Maine herself, Kim Hamlin is drawn to that smell, reminiscent of the outdoors, peaceful places, and the December holidays all at once. Her version of those gift-store sachets are knitted out of linen yarn and filled with balsam fir, a favorite choice for Christmas trees and wreaths.

These sachets are simple, fast, and versatile, the pattern being easily adapted to any size square you'd like. As shown here, they're perfect for drawers, closets, or mailing packages. Slightly bigger squares filled less full make aromatic coasters, and squares of any size can become throw pillows for the couch. Try experimenting with aromatic herbs, too—relaxing lavender is particularly appropriate for the holidays, bay leaves are sacred to the sun god Apollo (an important figure in solstice celebrations), and rosemary has the added benefit of keeping evil spirits at bay, according to superstitions of the Middle Ages.

FINISHED MEASUREMENTS
Approximately $3\frac{1}{2}$ ($4\frac{1}{4}$)" square

YARN
Louet Euroflax Originals (100% linen; 135 yards/ 50 grams): 1 skein and/or
Louet Euroflax Athens (100% linen; 200 yards / 100 grams): 1 skein
Note: Many sachets can be made from one skein.
Shown in: Originals #55 willow (pale green) and #50 sage (dark green), and in Athens #21026 moss lake (variegated light blue and pale green)

NEEDLES
One pair straight needles size US 4 (3.5 mm)
Change needle size if necessary to obtain correct gauge.

NOTIONS
Crochet hook size F/5 (3.75 mm)
Yarn needle, muslin or thin cloth for lining, sewing needle and thread, approximately 1 cup balsam fir tips (see Sources for Supplies, page 182)

GAUGE
22 sts and 38 rows = 4" (10 cm) in Garter stitch in Originals
20 sts and 38 rows = 4" (10 cm) in Garter stitch in Athens

Sachet

Front and Back (both alike)
CO 3 sts.
Increase Row: Knit across to last st, k1-f/b
in last st.
Repeat Increase Row until you have 25 (30) sts.
Decrease Row: Knit across to last 2 sts, k2tog.
Repeat Decrease Row until 3 sts remain;
BO remaining sts.

Lining
Cut two 4 (4¾)" squares out of muslin. Using
½" seam allowances, sew squares together
making sure to leave a small opening on one
side. Turn lining RS out (seams are now hidden
on the inside). Working over a bowl
to prevent spills, fill lining with balsam to your
liking. Whipstitch lining opening closed.

Finishing
Block knitted pieces to measurements. Place
one linen square on top of the other, making
sure diagonal ridges are going in the same
direction. With RS facing, using crochet hook
and working through both layers, single crochet
3 sides together, working 3 stitches into each
corner stitch; insert finished lining and single
crochet remaining side closed. Weave in ends.

SUZANNE ATKINSON *Evergreen and Christmas Rose Gift Bags*

Gift and wrapping all in one, these clever knitted bags feature two seasonal motifs—evergreen trees and Christmas roses—that lend themselves well to Fair Isle knitting in the round. They're offered in two sizes to fit a wide range of gifts, and either bag can easily double as a handbag. The bags are knit from the top down; the bottom panel is shaped with decreases to lie flat.

FINISHED MEASUREMENTS
Small Bag: Approximately 6½" in diameter by 8½" high
Large Bag: Approximately 7¾" in diameter by 11" high

YARN
Classic Elite Montera (50% wool / 50% llama; 127 yards / 100 grams):
Small bag: 1 skein each MC and CC
Shown in Christmas Rose pattern in #3832 magenta (MC) and #3888 fuchsia (CC)
Large bag: 2 skeins MC and 1 skein CC
Shown in Evergreen pattern in #3860 dark green (MC) and #3850 lime green (CC)

NEEDLES
One 16" (40 cm) circular (circ) needle size US 8 (5 mm)
One set of four or five double-pointed needles (dpn) size US 8 (5 mm)
Two double-pointed needles size US 7 (4.5 mm) for I-cord Ties
Change needle size if necessary to obtain correct gauge.

NOTIONS
Stitch marker, yarn needle

GAUGE
22 sts and 24 rows = 4" (10 cm) in Stockinette stitch (St st) color pattern using larger needles, after blocking

NOTES
✤ Numbers for working small Bag are listed first, with large Bag in ( ); if only one set of numbers is given, it applies to both sizes.
✤ The number of rows differs slightly between the Bags, depending on the color pattern used. Bags of same size are worked identically before and after the color patterns on the sides.
✤ Charts are worked from right to left for each round, beginning Rnd 1; work Chart repeat around entire piece.
✤ Use Jogless Color Change (see Special Techniques, page 175) to minimize the disruption of the color patterns.

Bag

Body
Using MC and circ needle, CO 100 (120) sts. Join for working in the rnd, being careful not to twist sts; place marker (pm) for beginning of rnd. Purl 1 rnd. Join CC.
Rnd 1: * K2 MC, k2 CC, repeat from * around.
Rnds 2–7: * K2 MC, p2 CC; repeat from * around; break off CC.
Knit 2 rnds using MC only.

Eyelet Rnd: * K8, BO 2 sts; repeat from * around.
Note: The st left on the needle after BO is included in k8.
Next Rnd: Knit, making 2 firm Backward Loop CO sts (see Special Techniques, page 174) over BO sts.
Knit even for 3 rnds.

CHRISTMAS ROSE PATTERN

Join CC, begin Chart 1; work Rnds 1–15 of
Chart, working 20-st repeat 5 (6) times around.
* Knit 2 rnds using MC only.
Next Rnd: Remove marker; k10, pm for new
beginning of rnd and begin Chart 1; work
Rnds 1–15 of Chart; repeat from * 0 (1) time.
Break off CC; knit 3 rnds using MC only.
Purl 1 rnd.

Shape Base

Rnd 1: * K18 (22), k2tog; repeat from *
around—95 (114) sts remain.
Rnd 2: * K17 (21), k2tog; repeat from *
around—90 (108) sts remain.
Rnd 3: * K16 (20), k2tog; repeat from *
around—85 (102) sts remain.
Continue as established, knitting one less st
before each decrease, until 5 (6) sts remain,
changing to dpn when the work no longer fits
on the circ needle.

Break off yarn, leaving several inches. Using
a blunt tapestry needle, thread yarn through
remaining sts and draw hole closed. Weave
end in securely on WS.

EVERGREEN PATTERN

Join CC, begin Chart 2; work Rnds 1–3
of Chart, working 5-st repeat 20 (24)
times around.
Knit 2 rnds using MC only.
Begin Chart 3; * work Rnds 1–12 of Chart,
working 10-st repeat 10 (12) times around.
Knit 2 rnds using MC only.
Next Rnd: Remove marker; k5, pm for new
beginning of rnd; repeat from * 1 (2) times.
Knit 2 rnds using MC only.
Begin Chart 2; work Rnds 1–3 of Chart.
Break off CC.
Knit 3 rnds using MC only.
Purl 1 rnd.

Shape Base

Work as for Christmas Rose
pattern Bag.

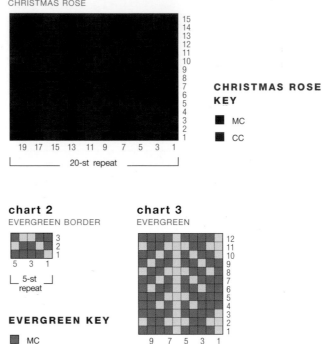

chart 1
CHRISTMAS ROSE

CHRISTMAS ROSE KEY

■ MC

■ CC

20-st repeat

chart 2
EVERGREEN BORDER

5-st repeat

chart 3
EVERGREEN

10-st repeat

EVERGREEN KEY

■ MC

□ CC

I-cord Ties (make 2 for each bag)
Using smaller dpn and CC, CO 3 sts.
Work I-cord (see Special Techniques, page 175)
for 36 (40)". BO by working sk2p. Break off yarn
and bring through last st to fasten off.
Weave in ends.

Finishing

To block, immerse Bag in a sink of cold water
and allow it to get very wet. Squeeze out excess
water, and place in an old towel of a similar
color. Gently squeeze out the rest of the excess
water. Place over a large coffee can or container
of similar dimensions, and allow it to dry.

When dry, weave one I-cord tie in and out
through eyelets and tie ends together.
Beginning at opposite side, weave other cord
in and out through eyelets in the opposite direction, and tie ends together.

Felted Wine Bags

A simple knitted tube, felted down to the size of a wine bottle, makes a very practical wine cozy or gift bag, especially festive when dressed up with stripes or embroidered snowflakes. From a more knitterly perspective, the bag can also be used to hold knitting needles; simply cut the top off an empty one-liter plastic drink bottle and slip it inside for added stability.

FINISHED MEASUREMENTS
Approximately 12¼" circumference by 13½" tall, after felting

YARN
Reynolds Lopi (100% Icelandic wool; 110 yards / 100 grams):
Solid bag: 1 skein #720 gold with #718 off-white embroidery
Striped bag: 1 skein each #209 pink, #315 brown, and #384 copper

NEEDLES
One set of five double-pointed needles (dpn) size US 11 (8 mm)
Change needle size if necessary to obtain correct gauge.

NOTIONS
Tapestry needle for embroidery, beads or crystals for snowflake version; leather strapping, approximately 4 yards heavy waxed thread to match leather (from shoe repair shop); and leather punch, for handle on striped version

GAUGE
11.2 sts and 13 rows = 4" (10 cm) in Stockinette stitch (St st) before felting
14 sts and 21 rows = 4" (10 cm) in Stockinette stitch (St st) after felting twice
Make a swatch and do a felting test before checking gauges.

Bags

Using color of choice, CO 40 sts; divide evenly on 4 needles. Join for working in the rnd, being careful not to twist sts; place marker (pm) for beginning of rnd.
Solid Bag: Knit even until piece measures 22" from the beginning.
Striped Bag: Work as for solid bag, changing colors every 7 rows, or as desired.
Note: To create neat stripes, follow the instructions on page 175 for Jogless Color Change.

Shape Base
Rnd 1: * K8, k2tog; repeat from * around— 36 sts remain.
Rnd 2: * K7, k2tog; repeat from * around— 32 sts remain.
Continue in this manner, knitting 1 less stitch before each decrease, until 8 sts remain. Break yarn, leaving a 12" tail; draw yarn through remaining 8 sts twice. Secure on WS and trim loose ends.

Felting

Turn Bag inside out and place in the washing machine. Wash using VERY HOT, SUDSY water, agitating on the longest cycle, then rinsing in VERY COLD water. Repeat, if necessary, checking progress every few minutes. Turn the Bag right side out. Shape the Bag, pulling and tugging hard as needed as the fabric is very sturdy.

Note: One-liter plastic soda bottles can be used to shape the Bag. Place the first bottle inside the Bag. Take a second empty bottle and cut off the top just below the curved part and place the lower part upside down over the first bottle to make a long tube. You can now stretch the Bag up along the sides of the soda bottles to the desired length of 13–14". It will shrink a bit as it dries.

Once the Bag is dry, embellish as desired.

Drawstring (snowflake version)

Make a crocheted chain or twisted cord (see Special Techniques, pages 174 or 178, respectively). With a wine bottle inside the Bag, tie the cord around the neck of the Bag to determine where to cut eight evenly spaced $\frac{1}{2}$" long slits for the drawstring. If this is your first felted project, don't be scared. The stitches will not come apart once the Bag is felted. With a sharp-pointed scissor, make your first slit, then measure around the Bag and divide the measurement by 8. For example: 12" circumference divided by 8 = $1\frac{1}{2}$" apart.

Handles, Closure Tab, and Tie
(striped version)

Cut leather strapping into two pieces in desired length for handles. Cut a piece of leather approximately 1" long for Tab Closure. Using a small leather punch, place two holes 1" apart and $\frac{1}{2}$" in from each end of the two Handles. Using waxed thread threaded on a needle, secure the straps to the Bag in a "figure 8," running the thread in and out of the holes. Attach closure Tab the same way. For the Tie, using single strand of waxed thread, finger knit or crochet a chain about 12" long, securing one end on side of the Bag opposite the Closure, about 1" down from the edge.

Inspired by a design in a vintage knitting book, Carrie Brenner has adapted a counterpane pattern into an updated "granny" bag, complete with bamboo handles and a coordinating accessories pouch (see page 164). The rugged, bulky handspun wool used for the bag offsets the femininity of the scallops. The pattern takes on a whole new feel when worked in a finer silk yarn for the smaller version, designed to be tucked into the carpet bag or carried on its own.

FINISHED MEASUREMENTS
Carpet Bag: Approximately 18" wide by 20" high without handles
Accessories Pouch: Approximately 11½" wide by 4½" high

YARN
Carpet Bag: La Lana Forever Random Blend (wool / mohair blend; 80 yards / 2 ounces): 10 skeins yellow brick road
Accessories Pouch: La Lana Wools Bombyx Silk (100% silk; approximately 300 yards / 6 ounces): burgundy

NEEDLES
Carpet Bag: One pair straight needles size US 10½ (6.5 mm)
Accessories Pouch: One pair straight needles size US 6 (4 mm)
Change needle size if necessary to obtain correct gauge.

NOTIONS
Yarn needle, ¾ (½) yard 45" wide lining fabric, sewing needle and thread
Carpet Bag: two 9" diameter bamboo handles
Accessories Pouch: 12–15" zipper

GAUGE
Carpet Bag: Each scallop = 5½" wide x 2½" high
Accessories Pouch: Each scallop = 3¾" wide x 2" high

NOTES
⊹ **P4-wrap:** P4, [return 4 sts to left-hand needle, bring yarn to back of work, slip 4 sts to right-hand needle, bring yarn to front of work] twice.

⊹ **Scallop Pattern**
(multiple of 21 sts + 5; 14-row repeat)
Note: St count changes from row to row; you can take an accurate count on Rows 1, 2, 12, 13, and 14.
Rows 1 and 3: Knit.
Row 2 (RS): Purl.
Row 4: K2, * yo, k21; repeat from * to last 3 sts, k3.
Row 5: P3, * [p1, k3] 5 times, p2; repeat from * to last 2 sts, p2.
Row 6: K2, * k1, yo, k1, [p3, k1] 5 times, yo; repeat from * to last 3 sts, k3.
Row 7: P3, * p2, [k3, p1] 5 times, p2; repeat from * to last 2 sts, p2.
Row 8: K2, * [k1, yo] 2 times, [ssk, p2] 5 times, [k1, yo] 2 times; repeat from * to last 3 sts, k3.
Row 9: P3, * p4, [k2, p1] 5 times, p4; repeat from * to last 2 sts, p2.
Row 10: K2, * [k1, yo] 4 times, [ssk, p1] 5 times, [k1, yo] 4 times; repeat from * to last 3 sts, k3.
Row 11: P3, * p8, [k1, p1] 5 times, p8; repeat from * to last 2 sts, p2.
Row 12: K2, * k8, [ssk] 5 times, k8; repeat from * to last 3 sts, k3.
Row 13: P3, * p8, p4-wrap, p9; repeat from * to last 2 sts, p2.
Row 14: Knit.
Repeat Rows 1–14 for desired length.

Handle Flap

Row 1 (RS): Knit.
Row 2: Purl.
Row 3: * K2tog; repeat from * across—
17 sts remain.
Rows 4–11: Work in St st.
Row 12 (WS): Turning Row—Knit.
Rows 13–20: Work in St st.
BO all sts.

Finishing

CARPET BAG

Slip Handle Flap through one handle, fold over at Turning Row and seam; repeat for other piece. With WS's together, seam sides and bottom of Bag. Cut 2 pieces fabric 18 ½" x 19". With RS's together, sew sides and bottom using ¼" seams. Baste pleats across top edge to fit opening. Fold top edge ¾" down to WS and press. Stitch lining to inside top edge of Bag below handles.

ACCESSORIES POUCH

Knit 2 rows, purl 1 row; BO all sts. Sew top edges of both pieces to sides of zipper. With WS together, seam sides and bottom of Pouch. Cut 2 pieces of fabric 12" x 5". With RS's together, sew sides and bottom using ¼" seams. Fold top edge ¼" down to WS and press. Stitch lining to inside of zipper tape, enclosing top end of zipper and leaving bottom end of zipper exposed (to be used as "handle"). Cut small piece of lining fabric and stitch to bottom end of zipper for finished look.

Bag (Pouch)

Back and Front (both alike)

Note: Instructions for Carpet Bag are given first; instructions for Accessories Pouch are shown in parentheses.
Using larger (smaller) needles, CO 68 (68) sts.
Work Rows 1–14 of Scallop pattern 5 (2) times.
If making Accessories Pouch, proceed to Finishing.

CARPET BAG

Work Rows 1–9 once more.
Row 10 (RS): K2, [k1, yo] 4 times, [(ssk, p1) 5 times, k8] 2 times, [ssk, p1] 5 times, [k1, yo] 4 times, k3—67 sts remain.
Row 11: P3, [p8, (k1, p1) 5 times] 3 times, p10.
Row 12: K10, [(ssk) 5 times, k8] 2 times, [ssk] 5 times, k11—52 sts remain.
Row 13: P12, [p4-wrap, p9] 3 times, p1.
Row 14: Knit.
Row 15: Purl.
BO 9 sts at beginning of next 2 rows—
34 sts remain.

HOLIDAY KNITTING STRATEGIES

We may love the idea of creating a special hand-wrought item for everyone on our gift lists, but transforming our good intentions into reality can take careful planning.

Prioritize
Choose one person on your list to knit for this year, and focus on that project alone. Then go down the list and pick next year's target.

Start early
Why scramble to make gifts in December when you can begin in August—or even January? Better yet, make one gift a month for an entire year. You may reach everyone on your list after all.

Think easy but personal
Throughout the year, using leftover yarn or stray skeins you couldn't resist buying from the sale bin, knit garter-stitch scarves. Then, when it's time to give a gift, personalize a scarf from your stash with simple embroidery, such as the recipient's name, initials, or a small holiday motif (as shown at left). Consider designating a knitting bag just for this purpose and keeping it easily accessible so that you remember to grab it whenever you think you'll have some spare time for easy knitting, such as when you are a passenger on a trip, sitting in the stands at a ball game, or waiting for an appointment.

Think small
A knitted sweater or throw may be the ultimate gift, but mittens, hats, pins, and other small items will also be well-appreciated and quicker to knit.

Tease
If you are planning to knit a larger gift for someone—or haven't finished one in time—wrap up your gauge swatch in a small box, perhaps with a photo or sketch of the intended gift. In addition to buying yourself some more time, you'll stretch the holiday spirit out a little farther—there's no reason you can't celebrate in July.

MICHELLE HEYMAN
Elf Caps

In the world of holiday spirits, there are elves and there are imps. We tend to think of elves as benevolent creatures—after all, they're the ones making Christmas goodies up at the North Pole. But imps are sprites of a different sort, famous for making mischief, and convenient scapegoats for all that goes awry in a holiday household. Whether they've been naughty or nice, your friends and family members will get a kick out of these quick-knit caps. You can make one in an afternoon with bulky yarn and big needles, customizing it with embellishments that suit the recipient's personality.

SIZES
Pointy Top Cap: X-Small (Small, Medium, Large)
To fit 6–18 months (2–4 years, 4 years–Adult Small, Adult Medium-Large)
Earflap Cap: Small (Medium, Large)
To fit 2–4 years, 4 years–Adult Small, Adult Medium-Large)

FINISHED MEASUREMENTS
Pointy-Top Cap:
Approximately 18 (20, 22, 24)" around
Earflap Cap:
Approximately 19 (21, 23)" around

YARN
Cascade Magnum (100% wool; 123 yards / 250 grams): 1 skein per cap
Shown in #9424 (pink), #4008 (burgundy), #9415 (dark green)

NEEDLES
One 16" circular (circ) needle size US 15 (10 mm)
One set of five double-pointed needles (dpn) size US 15 (10 mm)
Change needle size if necessary to obtain correct gauge.

NOTIONS
Crochet hook size N/5 (10 mm)
Stitch marker, yarn needle

GAUGE
8 sts and 11 rows = 4" (10 cm) in Stockinette stitch (St st)

Pointy-Top Cap

CO 36 (40, 44, 48) sts. Join for working in the rnd, being careful not to twist sts; place marker (pm) for beginning of rnd.

ROLLED-EDGE CAP
Work 5 (5, 6, 7)" in St st.

RIBBED-EDGE CAP
Work 3 rows k1, p1 rib; then work 4 (4½, 5, 5½)" in St st.

Shape Crown
Note: Change to dpn when the work no longer fits on the circ needle.
Size L: [Ssk, k10] 4 times—44 sts remain. Knit 1 row even.
Sizes M and L: [Ssk, k9] 4 times—40 sts remain. Knit 1 row even.
Sizes S, M, and L: [Ssk, k8] 4 times—36 sts remain. Knit 1 row even.
All sizes: [Ssk, k7] 4 times—32 sts remain. Knit 1 row even.
Continue as established, knitting one less st after each decrease, until 4 sts remain after finishing a knit row; ssk twice—2 sts remain.

Finishing
Break off yarn, leaving several inches. Using a yarn needle, thread yarn through remaining sts twice, draw tight, and secure on WS. Weave in ends.

Earflap Cap with braided ties and pompom and Pointy-Top Cap with ribbed edge.

Earflap Cap

Earflaps

Using dpn, CO 3 sts.

Row 1 and all odd numbered rows: Purl.

Row 2: K1, M1-L, k1, M1-R, k1—5 sts.

Row 4: K2, M1-L, k1, M1-R, k2—7 sts.

Row 6: K3, M1-L, k1, M1-R, k3—9 sts.

Row 8: Knit even.

Row 9: Purl even.

Leave first Earflap on needle, break yarn, leaving a 45" tail. Make second Earflap and leave on needle; break yarn leaving a 30" tail.

Joining Rnd

Note: Knit in ends of tails for a clean finish.

Using circ needle and new strand of yarn, knit 9 sts of the first Earflap; with the tail of yarn from the Earflap held in front, and the working yarn at the back, using the Long-Tail CO method (see Special Techniques, page 176), loosely CO 9 (11, 13) sts for Back of Cap; using working yarn, knit the 9 sts of the second Earflap; using the tail of yarn from the second Earflap and the working yarn, loosely CO 13 (15, 17) sts as for Back, for Front of Cap—40 (44, 48) sts.

Join for working in the rnd, being careful not to twist sts; place marker (pm) for beginning of rnd.

Ribbed Edge

Rnds 1–3: K9, p1, [k1, p1] 4 (5, 6) times, k9, p1, [k1, p1] 6 (7, 8) times. Change to St st.

Body of Cap

Work even until Cap measures 4 (4½, 5)" from Back CO edge.

Pointy-Top Cap with rolled edge (and a pair of pins for sparkle) and Earflap Cap with braided ties and embroidery.

Note: It's better to be a row short on the Cap length measurement rather than long, as there is plenty of height in this hat due to the pointed top; if it is too long, it will fall too low on the forehead.

Shape Top

Note: Change to dpn when the work no longer fits on the circ needle.

Size L: K3, [ssk, k10] 3 times, ssk, k7—44 sts remain.

Knit 1 row even.

Sizes M and L: K3, [ssk, k9] 3 times, ssk, k6—40 sts remain.

Knit 1 row even.

All Sizes: K3, [ssk, k8] 3 times, ssk, k5—36 sts remain.

Knit 1 row even.

Continue as established, working decrease rnd every rnd (omit work-even rnds), knitting one less st between decreases each rnd, until 4 sts remain.

Finishing

Break off yarn, leaving several inches. Using yarn needle, thread yarn through remaining sts twice, draw tight and secure on WS. Weave in ends.

Embellish (optional)

Using CC, embroider a simple shape, such as a leaf or snowflake, on each of the earflaps. Finish tip of Cap with Pompom or 4-Strand Braid Tie. Attach 4-Strand Braid Ties to each Earflap.

POMPOM

Using CC, make one 3" Pompom (see Special Techniques, page 176). Using crochet hook and 36" strand of CC, work crochet chain (see Special Techniques, page 174) for 4" or desired length; fasten off. Attach one end of chain to Pompom and one end to point of Cap.

4-STRAND BRAID TIES

Slip two 24" strands of yarn through the center stitch 1 or 2 rows up from the bottom edge of the Earflap. Place them so the back half of one strand is on the left, front half is center left; back half of other strand is on the right, front half is center right.

Step 1: Working left to right, take the left strand over the center left strand, then under the center right strand.

Step 2: Working right to left, take the right strand under the new center right strand, then over the new center left strand.

Repeat Steps 1 and 2 to desired length. Tie overhand knot to secure and cut ends to desired length for tassel.

Repeat for other Earflap.

Pointy-Top Cap with rolled edge.

Knit in a soft, chunky, and very warm alpaca yarn, this reversible kerchief hides what the designer calls "helmet head," hair smushed by a helmet during a day of skiing. It could easily do the same for a similar case of "bedhead."

FINISHED MEASUREMENTS
Approximately 18" wide, without ties

YARN
Blue Sky Alpaca Worsted Hand-Dye
(100% alpaca; 100 yards / 100 grams):
1 skein #2008 pearl pink

NEEDLES
One 24" circular needle size US 9 (5.5 mm)
Change needle size if necessary to obtain correct gauge.

GAUGE
16 sts and 20 rows = 4" (10 cm) in pattern

Kerchief

Note: Purl all yarnovers tbl on RS.
CO 3 sts.
Row 1 (WS): Knit.
Row 2: Knit.
Row 3: K1, M1, k1, M1, k1—5 sts.
Row 4: Knit.
Row 5: K2, M1, k1, M1, k2—7 sts.
Row 6 and all RS rows: K3, purl to last 3 sts, k3.
Row 7: K3, M1-L, k1, M1-R, k3—9 sts.
Row 9: K3, M1-L, k3, M1-R, k3—11 sts.
Row 11: K3, M1-L, ssk, yo, k1, yo, k2tog, M1-R, k3—13 sts.
Row 13: K3, M1-L, k1, ssk, yo, k1, yo, k2tog, k1, M1-R, k3—15 sts.
Row 15: K3, M1-L, k2, ssk, yo, k1, yo, k2tog, k2, M1-R, k3—17 sts.
Continue as established, increasing 2 sts every other row, until Kerchief measures 18" across—71 sts, ending with a RS row.
Knit 2 rows even.

Ties
First Tie: (WS) Knit across, turn; CO 24 sts using Cable CO method (see Special Techniques, page 174).
(WS) Knit across to the last st, slip the last stitch onto the right-hand needle.
DO NOT CUT YARN.
Second Tie: Using a separate strand of yarn approximately 60" long and Cable CO method, CO 24 sts onto the left-hand needle; return the slipped stitch to the left-hand needle.
Knit the first CO stitch before the slipped stitch, passing it over the slipped stitch as you knit it, then knit the slipped stitch (this will prevent a gap between the Tie and the Kerchief); continue to knit across the remaining 23 sts—119 sts.
Next Row (RS): Knit.
(WS) BO all sts knitwise.
Weave in loose ends.

La Luz Eye Mask

When the wrapping paper is put away and the last guests are gone, slip on this luxurious eye mask for some well-deserved post-holiday crashing. It's filled with lavender, which imparts relaxing aromatherapeutic qualities, and flax seed, which retains temperature well, so the mask can be popped into the microwave or refrigerated for a warm or cool treat. The smooth silk La Luz yarn feels wonderful on tired eyes—but it might feel even better sliding through your fingers as you knit it. The mask is also very easy to knit, offering a last-minute gift option that won't give you a headache. You can easily make two or three masks from one skein of La Luz.

FINISHED MEASUREMENTS
Approximately 10" wide by 5" high

YARN
Fiesta La Luz (100% silk; 210 yards / 2 ounces):
1 skein in Arctic Ice

NEEDLES
One pair straight needles size US 5 (3.75 mm)
Change needle size if necessary to obtain correct gauge.

NOTIONS
Stitch markers, yarn needle, 12" square muslin or other thin fabric for lining, sewing needle and thread, 1½ cups flax seed (available in bulk section of health food store), 1 cup dried lavender (see Sources for Supplies, page 182)

GAUGE
24 sts and 32 rows = 4" (10 cm) in Stockinette stitch (St st)

Eye Mask

Note: On RS (knit) rows, slip the stitch between the markers. This forms a fold line for the center of the mask. Do not slip on WS (purl) rows.

CO 37 sts.
Set-up Row: P18, place marker (pm), p1, pm, p18.
Row 1 (RS): K1, M1, knit to marker, sl 1, knit to last 3 sts, M1, k1—39 sts remain.
Row 2: Purl.
Row 3: Knit to marker, slip 1, knit to end of row.
Row 4: Purl.
Repeat Rows 1–4 three times more—45 sts after last Row 4.
Repeat Rows 1 and 2 five times—55 sts after last Row 2.
Repeat Rows 3 and 4 three times.
Row A: K1, k2tog-tbl, knit to marker, slip 1, knit to last 3 sts, k2tog, k1—53 sts remain.
Row B: Purl.
Repeat Rows A and B four times more—45 sts remain after last Row B.
Repeat Rows 1 and 2 five times—55 sts after last Row 2.
Repeat Rows 3 and 4 three times.
Repeat Rows A and B five times—45 sts remain after last Row B.
Row C: Knit to marker, slip 1, knit to end of row.
Row D: Purl.
Repeat Rows A–D three times—39 sts remain after last Row D.
Repeat Rows A and B once—37 sts remain after last Row B.
BO all sts, leaving a long tail for seaming.

Lining
Fold finished Eye Mask in half. Align fold of Eye Mask with edge of a piece of paper and trace shape; it doesn't have to be perfect, but flatten Mask enough to trace the curves correctly. Cut out mask template. Fold fabric in half with right sides together. Align straight edge of Mask template to folded edge of fabric and pin in place. Cut fabric ½" larger than template. Using ½" seam allowance, sew lining closed, following edge of template, leaving a 2" opening on one side. Remove template and turn right-side out through seam opening. Fill lining with lavender and flax. Sew lining closed. Sew Eye Mask closed around lining.

Special Techniques

Every knitter should have at least one or two really good reference books to help them learn new techniques as required for the projects they want to make. The techniques described here are not meant to replace a reference book. Rather, they are included to help in a pinch, for example, when you're knitting away from home and don't have access to your reference library or when the reference books you have don't include a particular technique needed for a project presented here. Most yarn stores stock a selection of reference titles. Take some time to browse through them to figure out which ones you like best—consider the way the information in them is presented as well as organized. Also ask fellow knitters which books they find most useful.

Backward Loop CO

Make a loop (using a slipknot) with the working yarn and place it on the right-hand needle [first st CO], * wind yarn around thumb clockwise, insert right-hand needle into the front of the loop on thumb, remove thumb and tighten st on needle; repeat from * for remaining sts to be CO, or for CO at the end of a row in progress.

Cable CO

Make a loop (using a slipknot) with the working yarn and place on the left-hand needle [first st CO], knit into slipknot, draw up a loop but do not drop st from left-hand needle; place new loop on left-hand needle; * insert the tip of the right-hand needle into the space between the last 2 sts on the left-hand needle and draw up a loop; place the loop on the left-hand needle. Repeat from * for remaining sts to be CO, or for CO at the end of a row in progress.

Crochet Chain

Make a slipknot and place on hook, * yarn over and draw through loop on hook; repeat from * for desired length.

Knitted Ornaments (see page 10).

Double-Start CO

This is a 2-st CO; the first st is made with a variation of the Long-Tail CO and the second is made with the Long-Tail CO. Leaving tail with about 1" of yarn for each st to be CO, make a slipknot in the yarn and place it on the right-hand needle (the slipknot is considered to be st 1). Insert the thumb and forefinger of your left hand between the strands of yarn so that the working end is around your forefinger, and the tail end is around your thumb "slingshot" fashion as for Long-Tail CO; now reverse the strand around your thumb so that the loop goes first around the outside of your thumb, with the tail coming down inside your hand and across your palm; insert the tip of the right-hand needle down under the back loop on the thumb, hook the strand coming from the forefinger by going over it back to front, and draw it through the loop on your thumb; remove your thumb from the loop and pull on the working yarn to tighten the new st on the right-hand needle; this is st 2. Now return your thumb and forefinger to their original Long-tail CO positions. Insert the tip of the right-hand needle into the front loop on the thumb, hook the strand of yarn coming from the forefinger from back to front, and draw it through the loop on your thumb; remove your thumb from the loop and pull on the working yarn to tighten the new st on the right-hand needle; this is st 1. Now return your thumb and forefinger to the variation CO positions. Repeat st 2 to complete the second pair, then work sts 1 and 2 for remaining sts to be CO.

Double-Strand CO

This may seem similar to Long-Tail CO in some ways; however, yarn is wound around the thumb in the opposite direction (counter-clockwise) and 2 strands are used instead of one.
Using 2 balls of yarn, leaving a long tail (approximately 1" for every st to be CO), make a slipknot with both strands, but pull one of the strands free, so that the slipknot has only one loop; place the loop on the right-hand needle (first CO st). Cut one of the strands attached to one of the balls; the remaining strands attached to the other ball will form the sts on the right-hand needle, the 2 tails will form a firm base for the sts.
Holding the 2 tails together as one, wrap them twice around your

Flower Pins shown clockwise from top: Morning Star, Pinwheel, Double Pinwheel, Morning Star, and Double Pinwheel (see page 152).

Duplicate Stitch

Duplicate st is similar to Kitchener st, except it is used for decorative purposes instead of joining two pieces together. Thread a yarn needle with chosen yarn and, leaving a tail to be woven in later, * bring the needle from WS to RS of work at the base of the st to be covered, pass the needle under both loops (the base of the st above) above the st to be covered; insert the needle into same place where you started (base of st), and pull yarn through to WS of work. Be sure that the new st is the same tension as the rest of the piece. Repeat from * for additional sts. A good way to visualize the path of the yarn for Duplicate st is to work a swatch in St st using main color (MC) for three rows, work 1 row alternating MC and a contrasting color, then work two additional rows using MC only.

Fringe

Using number of strands required in pattern, fold in half; with RS of piece facing, insert crochet hook just above edge to receive fringe, from back to front; catch the folded strands of yarn with the hook and pull through work to form a loop, insert ends of yarn through loop and pull to tighten.

Garter Stitch

Knit every row when working straight; knit 1 round, purl 1 round when working circular.

I-Cord

Using a double-pointed needle (dpn), CO or pick up the required number of sts; the working yarn will be at the left-hand side of the needle. * Transfer the needle with the sts to your left hand, bring the yarn around behind the work to the right-hand side; using a second dpn, knit the sts from right to left, pulling the yarn from left to right for the first st; do not turn. Slide the sts to the opposite end of the needle; repeat from * until the cord is the length desired. *Note: After a few rows, the tubular shape will become apparent.*

Intarsia Colorwork Method

Use a separate length of yarn for each color section. When changing colors, bring the new yarn up and to the right of the yarn just used to twist the yarns and prevent leaving a hole; do not carry colors not in use across the back of the work.

Jogless Color Change

To minimize the jog where colors change when working stripes in-the-round, work one round with the new color, remove beginning-of-the-round marker, lift the previous color st below the next new-color st onto the left-hand needle; k2tog (lifted st of previous-color and first st of new color), replace the marker. The beginning of the round will move 1 st to the left at each color change.

left thumb counter-clockwise (the ends of the tails will be to the back of your thumb, between your thumb and your palm); holding the single strand in your right hand, bring it to the front and over the right-hand needle to the back (forms a yo, the second CO st); insert right-hand needle into the double strand on your thumb, wrap yarn under and over the needle (the normal path to knit a st when working Conventional style); pull needle through the loops on thumb, forming a new st on the right-hand needle; repeat from * for number of sts to be CO. When you work the first row after CO, DO NOT knit into the back of the yarnovers; this will tighten them, reducing the elasticity of this CO. *Note: Due to the yo's in this CO, if the pattern requires an even number of sts, it will be necessary to CO 1 fewer st than needed in order to not end with a yo; to make up for the lost st, k1-f/b in second st on the first row to increase 1 st. If the pattern requires an odd number of sts, do not work the last yo.*

Kitchener Stitch

Using a blunt yarn needle, thread a length of yarn approximately 4 times the length of the section to be joined. Hold the pieces to be joined wrong sides together, with the needles holding the sts parallel, both ends pointing in the same direction. Working from right to left, * insert yarn needle in first st on front needle as if to knit, pull yarn through, remove st from needle; insert yarn needle into next st on front needle as if to purl, pull yarn through, leave st on needle; insert yarn needle into first st on back needle as if to purl, pull yarn through, remove st from needle; insert yarn needle into next st on back needle as if to knit, pull yarn through, leave st on needle. Repeat from *, working 3 or 4 sts at a time, then go back and adjust tension to match the pieces being joined. When 1 st remains on each needle, break yarn and pass through last 2 sts to fasten off.

Knitted CO

Make a loop (using a slipknot) with the working yarn and place it on the left-hand needle [first st CO], * knit into the st on the left-hand needle, draw up a loop but do not drop st from left-hand needle; place new loop on left-hand needle; repeat from * for remaining sts to be CO, or for casting on at the end of a row in progress.

Long-Tail CO

Leaving tail with about 1" of yarn for each st to be cast-on, make a slipknot in the yarn and place it on the right-hand needle. Insert the thumb and forefinger of your left hand between the strands of yarn so that the working end is around your forefinger, and the tail end is around your thumb "slingshot" fashion; * insert the tip of the right-hand needle into the front loop on the thumb, hook the strand of yarn coming from the forefinger from back to front, and draw it through the loop on your thumb; remove your thumb from the loop and pull on the working yarn to tighten the new st on the right-hand needle; return your thumb and forefinger to their original positions, and repeat from * for remaining sts to be CO.

Candy Cane Hats (see page 64).

Outline Stitch BO

Break off yarn, leaving a long tail (approximately 12" for every 10 sts to be BO); thread tail onto yarn needle. With RS facing, tail at left and above work, * insert needle into second st from left as if to knit and into first st as if to purl; pull yarn through and slip first st off the needle. Repeat from * until all sts have been BO, keeping the tension fairly loose; it may be tightened later.

Pompom

You can use a pompom maker or the following method: Cut 2 cardboard circles in the diameter of the pompom desired. Cut a 1" diameter hole in the center of each circle. Cut away a small wedge out of each circle to allow for wrapping yarn. Hold the circles together with the openings aligned. Wrap yarn tightly around the circles. Carefully cut yarn around outer edge of the cardboard circles. Using a 12" length of yarn, wrap around strands between the 2 circles and tie tightly. Slip the cardboard circles off the completed pompom; trim pompom, leaving the ends of the tie untrimmed. Using ends of tie, sew pompom to garment.

Provisional CO

Using waste yarn, CO the required number of sts; work in St st for 3–4 rows; work 1 row with a thin, smooth yarn, (crochet cotton or ravel cord used for machine knitting) as a separator; change to main yarn and continue as directed. When ready to work the live sts, pull out the separator row, placing the live sts on a spare needle.

Provisional (Crochet Chain) CO

Using a crochet hook and smooth yarn (crochet cotton or ravel cord used for machine knitting), work a crochet chain with a few more chains than the number of sts needed; fasten off. If desired, tie a knot on the fastened-off end to mark the end that you will be unraveling from later. Turn the chain over; with a needle 1 size smaller than required for piece and working yarn, starting a few chains in from the beginning of the chain, pick up and knit one st in each bump at the back of the chain, leaving any extra chains at the end unworked.
Change to needle size required for project on first row.
When ready to work the live sts, unravel the chain by loosening the fastened-off end and "unzipping" the chain, placing the live sts on a spare needle.

Reading Charts

Unless otherwise specified in the instructions, Charts are read from right to left for RS rows, from left to right for WS rows when working straight; the numbers will indicate whether the Chart is to begin with a RS or WS row. All rounds are read from right to left when working circular.

Reverse Stockinette Stitch (Rev St st)

Purl on RS rows, knit on WS rows when working straight; purl every round when working circular.

Ribbing

Although Rib st patterns use different numbers of sts, all are worked in the same way, whether straight (in rows) or in-the-round. The instructions will specify how many sts to knit or purl; the example below uses k1, p1.

Row/Rnd 1: * K1, p1; repeat from * across (end k1 if an odd number of sts).

Row/Rnd 2: Knit the knit sts and purl the purl sts as they face you.

Repeat Row/Rnd 2 for Rib st.

Seed Stitch

Row/Rnd 1:* K1, p1; repeat from * across (end k1 if an odd number of sts).

Row/Rnd 2: Knit the purls and purl the knits as they face you.

Repeat Row/Rnd 2 for Seed st.

Short Row Shaping

Work the number of sts specified in the instructions, wrap and turn [wrp-t] as follows:

Bring yarn to the front (purl position), slip the next st purlwise to the right-hand needle, bring yarn to back of work, return slipped st on right-hand needle to left-hand needle; turn, ready to work the next row, leaving remaining sts unworked.

When Short Rows are completed, or when working progressively longer Short Rows, work the wrap together with the wrapped st as you come to it as follows:

If st is to be worked as a knit st, insert the right-hand needle into the wrap, from beneath the wrap up, then into the wrapped st; k2tog; if st to be worked is a purl st, insert needle into the wrapped st, then down into the wrap; p2tog. (Wrap may be lifted onto the left-hand needle, then worked together with the wrapped st if this is easier.)

Stockinette Stitch (St st)

Knit on RS rows, purl on WS rows when working straight; knit every round when working circular.

Stranded (Fair Isle) Colorwork Method

When more than one color is used per row, carry color(s) not in use loosely across the WS of work. Be sure to secure all colors at beginning and end of rows to prevent holes.

Tassel

Using color of your choice, wind yarn 20 times (or to desired thickness) around a piece of cardboard or other object the

Pompom Garland (see page 14).

same length as desired for Tassel. Slide yarn needle threaded with matching yarn under the strands at the top of the Tassel; tie tightly, leaving ends long enough for attaching Tassel to garment. Cut through all strands at the opposite end. Tie a second piece of yarn tightly around the Tassel several times, approximately $\frac{1}{2}$" from top of Tassel; secure ends inside top of Tassel. Trim ends even; attach to garment.

Three-Needle BO

Place the sts to be joined onto two same-size needles; hold the pieces to be joined with the right sides facing each other and the needles parallel, both pointing in the same direction (to the right). Holding both needles in your left hand, using working yarn and a third needle same size or one size larger, insert third needle into first st on front needle, then into first st on back needle; knit these two sts together; * knit next st from each needle together (two sts on right-hand needle); pass first st over second st to BO one st. Repeat from * until one st remains on third needle; cut yarn and fasten off.

Tubular BO

This BO requires 2 or more rows of Tubular Stockinette stitch (Tubular St st) before working the actual BO; the edge will be firmer if Tubular St st is done with needles 1 or 2 sizes smaller than size used for ribbing. Work 3 to 5 rows (rnds) in Tubular St st (see page 178), unless instructed otherwise.

After working Tubular St st, you now have 2 independent layers of fabric on the same needle. If desired, they may be separated onto 2 needles (knit sts on one needle, purl sts on another) and grafted using Kitchener st (see page 176); if left on one needle, work as follows:

Cut yarn, leaving a tail about 4 times the length of edge to be BO (if a large area is to be grafted and the yarn is inclined to fray, it may be necessary to do this in small sections, weaving ends in on wrong side as you go).

Thread tail on a yarn needle. As you work, do not pull the yarn too tightly, try to match the tension of the rest of the knitting; work 3 or 4 sts, then go back and adjust tension if necessary; insert yarn needle into first st on the left-hand needle as if to knit, remove it from the needle; insert yarn needle as if to purl in front of work into third st (now the second st remaining on the left-hand needle) and pull yarn through; insert yarn needle as if to purl into the second st (now the first st remaining on the left-hand needle), and remove it from the needle; working around the back of the third st (now the first st on the left-hand needle), insert the yarn needle into the fourth st (now the second st on left-hand needle) as if to knit and pull the yarn through. Repeat from * until you have BO all sts; pull tail through the remaining st and fasten off.

Tubular CO

This CO requires 2 or more rows of Tubular Stockinette stitch (see below) after the CO and before beginning the ribbing; the edge will be firmer if Tubular St st is done with needles 1 or 2 sizes smaller than size to be used for ribbing.

Using ribbing size needles, waste yarn, and using Backward Loop CO (see page 174), CO half the number of sts required (plus 1 if an odd number of sts is required); (if desired, knit 1 row with crochet cotton or ravel cord to make it easier to remove waste yarn later); break yarn. Using larger needles and working yarn, [k1, p1] in each st or [* k1, yo; rep from * across], doubling the number of sts. *Note: If you require an odd number of sts and are working back and forth, knit the last st (DO NOT double it). If you are working in the round, double the st; you will need to decrease 1 st on the first row after ribbing to return to an odd number of sts.*

Work per instructions or work Tubular St st for 2–4 rows.

Change to ribbing size needles and work for length desired in 1x1 ribbing, or as instructed in the pattern. Remove waste yarn from beginning by pulling ravel cord, or unravel waste yarn.

Tubular Stockinette Stitch

Two or more rows (rnds) of Tubular St st are required after working Tubular CO or before working Tubular BO. For working back and forth: Row 1: * K1, slip 1 wyif; repeat from * across (end k1 if an odd number of sts). Row 2: (Slip 1 wyif if an odd number of sts) * K1, slip 1 wyif; repeat from * across. For working in-the-round: Rnd 1: * K1, slip 1 wyif; repeat from * around. Rnd 2: * Slip 1 wyib, p1; repeat from * around. Repeat Rows

Zigzag Poncho (see page 112).

(Rnds) 1 and 2 as specified in the pattern. *Note: If working before Tubular BO and after 1 or more rows of 1x1 rib, you will be knitting the knit sts and slipping the purl sts on every row.*

Twisted Cord

Fold one strand (or number of strands specified in the pattern) of yarn in half and secure the loose strands together to a stationary object. Twist from other end until the yarn begins to buckle. Fold twisted length in half and holding ends together, allow to twist up on itself. Tie the end in your hand with an overhand knot to secure.

Yarnover (yo) at beginning of a row

If first st is to be knit, hold yarn to the front (in front of needle with no sts), insert needle into first st to be worked, bring yarn over the needle and knit; if the first st is to be purled, bring yarn around the needle from front to back, then to front (purl position) and purl. Be careful not to lose the yo; it can easily slip out of position.

Yarnover (yo) other than beginning of row

Bring yarn forward (to the purl position), then place it in position to work the next st. If next st is to be knit, bring yarn over the needle and knit; if next st is to be purled, bring yarn over the needle and then forward again to the purl position and purl. Work the yo in pattern on the next row unless instructed otherwise.

Abbreviations

BO = Bind off

Circ = Circular

CC = Contrast color

CO = Cast on

Dc (double crochet) = Working from right to left, yarn over hook (2 loops on hook), insert hook into the next st, yarn over hook and pull up a loop (3 loops on hook), [yarn over and draw through 2 loops] twice.

Dcd (double centered decrease) = Slip next 2 sts together knitwise to right-hand needle, k1, pass 2 slipped sts over knit st.

Dpn(s) = Double-pointed needle(s)

Hdc (half double crochet) = Yarn over hook (2 loops on hook), insert hook into next st, yarn over hook and draw up a loop (3 loops on hook), yarn over and draw through all 3 loops on hook.

K = Knit

K2tog = Knit 2 sts together.

K3tog = Knit 3 sts together.

K1-f/b = Knit into front loop and back loop of same st to increase one st.

MC = Main color

M1-R (make 1-right slanting) = With the tip of the left-hand needle inserted from back to front, lift the strand between the two needles onto the left-hand needle; knit it through the front loop to increase one st.

M1 or M1-L (make 1-left slanting) = With the tip of the left-hand needle inserted from front to back, lift the strand between the two needles onto the left-hand needle; knit the strand through the back loop to increase one st.

M1P (make 1 purlwise) = With the tip of the left-hand needle inserted from back to front, lift the strand between the two needles onto the left-hand needle; purl the strand through the front loop to increase one st.

P = Purl

P1-f/b = Purl the next st through the front of its loop, then through the back of its loop, to increase one st.

Pm = Place marker

Psso (pass slipped stitch over) = Pass slipped st on right-hand needle over the st(s) indicated in the instructions, as in binding off.

Rnd = Round

RS = Right side

Sc (single crochet) = Insert hook into next st and draw up a loop (2 loops on hook), yarn over and draw through both loops on hook.

Skp (slip, knit, pass) = Slip next st knitwise to right-hand needle, k1, pass slipped st over knit st.

Sk2p (double decrease) = Slip next st knitwise to right-hand needle, k2tog, pass slipped st over st from k2tog.

Sl (slip) = Slip stitch(es) as if to purl, unless otherwise specified.

Sl st (crochet slip stitch) = Insert hook in st, yarn over hook, and draw through loop on hook.

Sm = Slip marker

Ssk (slip, slip, knit) = Slip the next 2 sts to the right-hand needle one at a time as if to knit; return them back to left-hand needle one at a time in their new orientation; knit them together through the back loops.

Sssk = Same as ssk, but worked on next 3 sts.

Ssp (slip, slip, purl) = Slip the next 2 sts to right-hand needle one at a time as if to knit; return them to the left-hand needle one at a time in their new orientation; purl them together through the back loops.

St(s) = Stitch(es)

K1-tbl = Knit one st through the back loop, twisting the st.

Tbl = Through the back loop

Tog = Together

WS = Wrong side

Wrp-t = Wrap and turn *(see Special Techniques—Short Row Shaping)*

Wyib = With yarn in back

Wyif = With yarn in front

Yo = Yarnover *(see Special Techniques)*

Contributors

SUSAN ALAIN

Susan is a painter who has studied art in Montreal and Rome, and a fiber artist who knits and spins purely for fun.

SUZANNE ATKINSON

Suzanne began designing after completing the Master Knitter Program of the Knitting Guild of Canada, and since then her work has been published in the book *Kids, Kids, Kids* (XRX) and in *Knitter's* magazine.

VÉRONIK AVERY

Véronik's designs have been published in *Interweave Knits* and the Web magazine *Knitty.com* and in the books *Weekend Knitting* (Stewart, Tabori & Chang) and *Knit Wit* (HarperResource). She is currently working on a book of her designs for Stewart, Tabori & Chang. Visit her website at www.veronikavery.com.

BETTY CHRISTIANSEN

Betty's writing has been featured in several knitting magazines as well as *KnitLit, Too* (Three Rivers) and *For the Love of Knitting* (Voyageur), and her designs have appeared in *Vogue Knitting* and *JoAnn etc*. She has an MFA in writing from Sarah Lawrence College in New York.

AMANDA BLAIR BROWN

Amanda has toured with the American Repertory Theatre, taught Latin, and worked as an assistant producer on a documentary film about the American military industrial complex. Her designs have appeared in *Interweave Knits*.

CARRIE BRENNER

A sort of knitting spokesperson, Carrie has taught at Make Workshop in New York City, has appeared on the Fine Living cable TV program *Back to Basics*, and has been featured in knitting articles in *Newsweek* and *Time Out New York*.

CYNTHIA CRESCENZO

A knitter for more than twenty years, Cynthia enjoys exploring all types of knitting techniques and yarn types. She is the owner of Knitting Central in Westport, Connecticut.

SANDY CUSHMAN

Sandy is a graduate of the Rhode Island School of Design, where she studied painting and textiles and dabbled in knitting. Her designs have been published by *Interweave Knits* and Berocco.

TEVA DURHAM

Teva's designs and writing have been featured in major knitting magazines as well as many books, including *Weekend Knitting* (Stewart, Tabori & Chang), *Scarf Style* (Interweave), and *For the Love of Knitting* (Voyageur). She is the author of *Loop-d-Loop: More than 40 Novel Designs for Knitters* (Stewart, Tabori & Chang). Visit her website at www.loop-d-loop.com.

NICKY EPSTEIN

Nicky has gained worldwide recognition for her innovative work, whimsical sense of style, and informative workshops. Her designs have been featured in many knitting magazines and books, on television, and in museums. She is the author of numerous books, including *Knitted Embellishments*, *Knitting for Your Home*, *Knits for Barbie Doll*, *Crochet for Barbie Doll*, *Knitting on the Edge*, *Barbie and Me*, and *Knitting over the Edge*.

NORAH GAUGHAN

For almost twenty years, Norah has worked as a freelance designer throughout the handknitting industry and has designed pattern stitches for the garment industry. For six years, beginning in the mid-nineties, she was design director of Reynolds, Artful Yarns, and Adrienne Vittadini Yarns. She is currently working on a book of her designs for Stewart, Tabori & Chang.

PRISCILLA GIBSON-ROBERTS

Priscilla specializes in socks, lace knitting, and knitting and spinning traditions. She has authored numerous magazine articles and books on these topics, including *Knitting in the Old Way* (Nomad), *Simple Socks*, *Plain and Fancy* (Nomad), *High Whorling* (Nomad), *Salish Indian Sweaters* (Interweave), and *Ethnic Socks & Stockings* (XRX).

KIM HAMLIN

Knitting became Kim's passion while she was earning her BA in dance and visual arts at Bennington College. Her work appears in *Last-Minute Knitted Gifts* (Stewart, Tabori & Chang).

MICHELLE HEYMAN

A graduate of the Rhode Island School of Design, Michelle has worked in the commercial knitwear world for twenty years, doing technical design for J. Crew, Ann Taylor, Tahari, and Antonio Melani.

PENNEY KOLB

After winning a Brown Sheep Company design competition, Penney decided to take knitting more seriously. Her work has since appeared in *Twists and Turns: The Newsletter for Lovers of Cable Knitting* and in her own line of knitting patterns, *Sheep Thrills*.

FAINA LETOUTCHAIA

Faina has spent most of her life in St. Petersburg, Russia, where her mother taught her to knit as a very young girl. She credits her understanding of fit and fine finishing to her grandmother, a professional tailor and dressmaker trained in the European tradition of haute couture. Her designs have appeared in *Interweave Knits*.

ROBIN MELANSON

Robin learned to knit when she was eight, and has always made her own clothes. Her designs have appeared in *Interweave Knits, Knitter's,* and *Family Circle Easy Knitting*. She works part-time in a yarn store.

NANCY MINSKY

Nancy is an award-winning graduate of Parsons School of Design and the New School of Social Research. Her design credits include jobs as assistant fashion designer at Calvin Klein, then the head of various design departments there. She established the Paul Alexander line, and has taught fashion sketching at Parsons.

ANNIE MODESITT

Known for her unorthodox projects and techniques, Annie has contributed designs to numerous knitting magazines, websites, films, and yarn companies, and to the books *Weekend Knitting* (Stewart, Tabori & Chang) and *Stitch 'n Bitch* (Workman). She is the author of *Confessions of a Knitting Heretic* (ModeKnit Press).

JILLIAN MORENO

Inspired by art, fashion, and pop culture, Jillian knits and designs knitwear fanatically. She is a frequent contributor to the Web knitting magazine *Knitty.com*.

KATHY PASUSTA

A designer and hand-dyer for Blue Sky Alpacas, Kathy knits, spins, weaves, and raises sheep and llamas. She also creates a line of all-natural soaps, lotions, and cleaning products, which she sells under the brand name Shepherd's Choice.

LEIGH RADFORD

An award-winning graphic designer and the art director for *Interweave Knits*, Leigh loves to experiment with new ways to work with fiber. Her designs appear regularly in *Interweave Knits* and have also been published by *Fiber Trends, Classic Elite Yarns,* and *Louet Sales*. Leigh is the author of *AlterKnits* (Stewart, Tabori & Chang). Visit her website at www.leighradford.com or www.alterknits.net.

MICHELE ROSE ORNE

Michele has designed knitwear for major retailers such as Ann Taylor, Talbot's, Nautica, Lord & Taylor, and Casual Corner. Her designs have appeared in many knitting magazines and in books such as *Vogue Knitting's American Collection* (Sixth & Spring) and *Knitting in America* (Artisan).

LESLIE SCANLON

A longtime knitting teacher, Leslie has designed for *Classic Elite, Blue Sky Alpacas, Frog Tree Alpaca,* and *Interweave Knits* magazine. She also sells her patterns through her knitwear company MAC & ME. She and her husband own a hotel on the ocean in Maine, where they host knitting weekends every fall.

IRIS SCHREIER

Iris comes from a line of fiber artists and couturiers that extends back to her great-grandparents. She is the author of *Exquisite Little Knits* and *Modular Knits* (both from Lark). She also sells her handpainted yarns under the name Artyarns (www.artyarns.com).

JO SHARP

Jo is a handknit designer based in Fremantle, Western Australia, whose collections feature her own luxury hand-knitting yarns in natural fibers such as wool, cotton, silk, and cashmere in rich, earthy tones. Visit her website at www.josharp.com.au.

CINDY TAYLOR

Cindy is a fourth-generation knitter. Since 1987, she has been designing knitwear for the retail market, specializing in a bold yet feminine style influenced by her background in visual and graphic art. She is also an instructor, having taught most recently in the fashion department at Virginia Commonwealth University.

JOLENE TREACE

JoLene is a designer and part-time registered nurse. She has designed patterns for Louet Sales, Jamieson's *Shetland Knitting Book 2* (Unicorn), and the British magazine *Knitting*. Her self-published patterns are sold through Black Water Abbey.

GINA WILDE

Gina is the co-founder and artistic director for Alchemy Yarns of Transformation (www.alchemyyarns.com).

ANNE WOODBURY

Anne's designs, most notably for socks, have appeared in *Interweave Knits, Cast On, Heels & Toes Gazette, InKnitters,* and the Web magazine *KnitNet*. She's also designed patterns for Himalaya Yarn.

Sources for Supplies

Alchemy Yarns
PO Box 1080
Sebastopol, CA 95473
707-823-3276
www.alchemyyarns.com

ArtfulYarns/JCA/Reynolds
35 Scales Ln.
Townsend, MA 01469
978-597-8794

Artyarns
39 Westmoreland Ave.
White Plains, NY 10606
914-428-0333
www.artyarns.com

Berroco
14 Elmdale Rd., PO Box 367
Uxbridge, MA 01569
800-343-4948
www.berroco.com

Black Water Abbey Yarns
PO Box 470688
Aurora, CO 80047
720-320-1003
www.abbeyyarns.com

Blue Sky Alpacas, Inc.
PO Box 387
St. Francis, MN 55070
888-460-8862
www.blueskyalpacas.com

Brown Sheep Company
100662 County Rd. 16
Mitchell, NE 69357
800-826-9136
www.brownsheep.com

Cascade Yarns
1224 Andover Park East
Tukwila, WA 98188
800-548-1048
www.cascadeyarns.com

Classic Elite Yarns
122 Western Ave.
Lowell, MA 01851
800-343-0308
www.classiceliteyarns.com

Debbie Bliss Yarns
Dist. by Knitting Fever
35 Debevoise Ave.
Roosevelt, NY 11575
800-645-3457
www.knittingfever.com

Fiesta Yarns
4583 Corrales Rd.
Corrales, NM 87048
505-892-5008
www.fiestayarns.com

Filatura di Crosa
Dist. by Tahki/Stacy Charles, Inc.
8000 Cooper Ave., Bldg 1
Glendale, NY 11385
800-338-YARN
www.tahkistacycharles.com

Fire Mountain Gems (beads)
1 Fire Mountain Way
Grants Pass, OR 97526
800-355-2137
www.firemountaingems.com

Goddess Yarns
2911 Cavanaugh Blvd.
Little Rock, AR 72205
866-332-YARN
www.goddessyarns.com

Great Adirondack Yarns
950 County Hwy. 126
Amsterdam, NY 12010
518-843-3381
www.dknitting.com

Haneke Wool Fashions
630 N. Black Cat Rd.
Meridian, ID 83642
800-523-9665

Harrisville Designs
Center Village, PO Box 806
Harrisville, NH 03450
800-338-9415
www.harrisville.com

Kimmet Croft Fibers
5850 Schudy Rd.
Wisconsin Rapids, WI 54495
888-264-8740
www.fairyhare.com

La Lana Wools
136-C Paseo Norte
Taos, NM 87571
505-758-9631
www.lalanawools.com

The Lavender Fields
(organic lavender)
12460 Keys Creek Rd.
PO Box 2162
Valley Center, CA 92082
888-407-1489
www.thelavenderfields.com

Louet Sales
808 Commerce Park Dr.
Ogdensburg, NY 13669
613-925-4502
www.louet.com

Maine Balsam Fir Products
(balsam fir tips)
PO Box 9
West Paris, ME 04289
1-800-522-5726
www.mainebalsam.com

Manos del Uruguay
Dist. by Design Source
PO Box 770
Medford, MA 02155
888-566-9970

Mission Falls
Dist. by Unique Kolours
28 N. Bacton Hill Rd.
Malvern, PA 19355
800-25-2DYE4
www.uniquekolours.com

Mountain Colors
4072 Eastside Hwy.
Stevensville, MT 59870
406-777-3377
www.mountaincolors.com

Muench Yarns
1323 Scott St.
Petaluma, CA 94954
800-733-9276
www.muenchyarns.com

Needful Yarns Inc.
4476 Chesswood Dr.
Toronto, ON M3J2B9
Canada
OR
60 Industrial Pkwy. PMB #233
Cheektowaga, NY 14227
866-800-4700
www.needfulyarnsinc.com

Out on a Whim (beads)
121 E. Cotati Ave.
Cotati, CA 94931
707-664-8343
www.whimbeads.com

Rowan
Dist. by Westminster Fibers
4 Townsend West, Unit 8
Nashua, NH 03063
603-886-5041
www.knitrowan.com

The blouses on pages 117 and 143 and the jacket and skirt on page 153 are from **Avolon**, 4341 Irvington Rd., Irvington, VA 22480; 804-438-6793; www.shopavolon.com.

Acknowledgments

During the year I spent working on *Handknit Holidays*, I had a lot of distracting demands on my time, both personal and professional. Without the support of an amazing circle of colleagues, friends, and volunteer knitters, I would never have completed it. Throughout the process, they made me feel very fortunate to have them on my side.

Betty Christiansen provided the glue that holds the book together by collaborating with me on nearly every aspect of it. She consistently quelled my worries by always working to her own high standards and by being such a caring friend. Susan Pittard took on the enormous job of photographing the projects and maintained her commitment to excellence even when the job threatened to overwhelm all of us. Thanks to her and to Joelle Hoverson, who introduced Susan and me and also shared her yarn shop, Purl (www.purlsoho.com), as well as her apartment for photography. Shelly Coon did a fabulous job with the prop-styling, often creating holiday magic in an empty corner or on a bare table. Wardrobe stylist Daria Maneche came to the rescue for the last shoot at Louise Allen's home (thank you, Louise), providing just the right touch of holiday glamour. Graphic designer Lana Lê went far beyond the call of duty. In addition to designing the exquisite pages before you, she also pitched in to help whenever possible, whether we needed her to find models or locations, drive a crew of people to a meeting, or embroider a flower on a scarf. Eve Ng, Dee Neer, and Sue McCain took on the daunting task of tech-editing the over-fifty projects in *Handknit Holidays*.

Of course, there would be no book without the designers whose projects are showcased. Thanks to Amy Singer of Knitty.com for posting news of this project and, thus, introducing me to a new wealth of talent and creativity. And thanks to all the designers with whom I've worked before and who have been so loyal, especially Véronik Avery, Sandy Cushman, Teva Durham, Nicky Epstein, Norah Gaughan, Priscilla Gibson-Roberts, Robin Melanson, Annie Modesitt, Leigh Radford, Cindy Taylor, Michele Orne, and Jo Sharp. Thanks to Michelle Heyman for finding me all these years after high school, for sharing her designs, and for introducing me to Nathalie and Larry Appel. And thanks to Nathalie and Larry for letting us descend upon their beautiful home for several days of photography. Thanks again to Cindy Taylor for sharing her creative ideas and enthusiasm and for responding to my last-minute call for clothing for photography at the Appel's with her usual vigor and flair—especially amazing this time as she was in the middle of a move. For clothing, Cindy called upon her friend Sonja Smith and Sonja's very special boutique Avolon (www.shopavolon.com).

I am grateful to the many volunteers that Betty Christiansen rounded up in Wisconsin and beyond to knit extra squares for the Community Afghan, Signature Scarves, Flower Pins, and other projects. They are Barb Katrana, Linda Miles, Melody Jane Moore, Michelle Mott, Jane Radloff, Rita Ross, Linda Sherony (Forest Gansey), Chris Swain (Candy Cane Hats), Suzanne Toce, Mary Veldy (Wisconsin Winter Shawl), Janet Virata, and Peg Zappen.

I am also indebted to the *Handknit Holidays* team of models. They are Jeremy Balderson, Jennifer Bryan Bremmer, Norah Colie, Pam Cook, Jason Bremmer, Laura Dever, Harriet Franke, Marie-Theres Franke, Gavin Hall, Conor Hartley, Stephanie Jordan, Deidra Lane, Matt Low, Clay Ross, Ava Syed, and Zoraida Walker. A special thanks to Marie and Pam, who in between looking great for the camera, vacuumed, washed dishes, packed up boxes, and basically did whatever we needed, no matter how unglamorous.

At Stewart, Tabori & Chang I am in the unusual position of being both a full-time editor and an author. To my coworkers there, thanks so much for your support and warmth and enthusiasm for knitting. A special thanks to Meryl Jacobs, who reached out to me when I really needed a hand, and to Marisa Bulzone, Beth Huseman, Jennifer Eiss, and Dervla Kelly, who helped to lighten my workload during stressful times. As always, a huge thank you goes to publisher Leslie Stoker for her confidence, loyalty, and compassion.

Sparkly Kiss Cap (see page 108).

Index